DECORATING FURNITURE

■

TEXTURE, PAINT, ORNAMENT AND MOSAIC PROJECTS

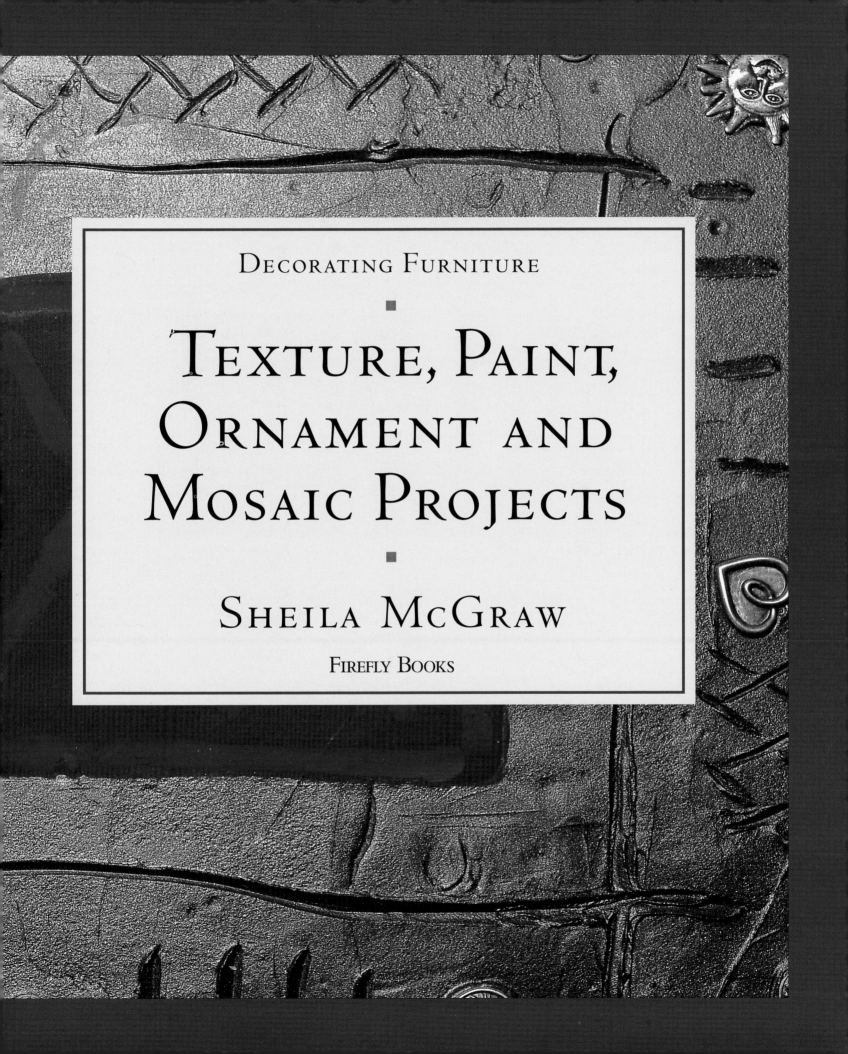

Decorating Furniture

Texture, Paint, Ornament and Mosaic Projects

Sheila McGraw

Firefly Books

A FIREFLY BOOK

Published by Firefly Books Ltd. 2002

National Library of Canada Cataloguing in Publication Data

McGraw, Sheila
Texture, paint, ornament and mosaic projects / Sheila McGraw.

(Decorating furniture)
ISBN 1-55297-618-1

1. Furniture painting.   2.   Decoration and ornament.
I. Title.   II. Series.

TT199.4.M339 2002   745.7   C2002-901440-9

Publisher Cataloging-in-Publication Data (U.S.)

McGraw, Sheila.
   Decorating furniture: texture, paint, ornament and mosaic projects
/ Sheila McGraw. – 1st ed.

[128] p. : col. photos. ; cm.   (Decorating Furniture)
Summary: A step-by-step guide to furniture finishes including tools
and materials, processes and projects.

ISBN 1-55297-618-1 (pbk.)

1. Furniture finishing.   2. Furniture painting.   3. Decoration and
ornament.   I. Title.   II. Series.

745.7/ 23 21   CIP   TT199.4.M34 2002

Text by Sheila McGraw
Photography and cartoon illustrations by Sheila McGraw
Design by Sheila McGraw and Counterpunch/Linda Gustafson
Page production by Counterpunch

Published by   Published in the U.S. by
Firefly Books Ltd.   Firefly Books (U.S.) Inc.
3680 Victoria Park Avenue   P.O. Box 1338, Ellicott Station
Willowdale, Ontario   Buffalo, New York 14205 USA
Canada M2H 3K1

Printed and bound in Canada by Friesens
Altona, Manitoba

*The Publisher acknowledges the financial support of the Government of Canada through
the Book Publishing Industry Development Program for its publishing activities.*

To my husband, Lionel

Acknowledgments

Thank you to everyone who worked with me on this book: Lionel Koffler for making the book possible; Pamela Anthony, Melanie Siegel and Pauline McGraw-Pike for their assistance, and for lending their hands for photography. Also to Max Piersig and Jason Wing for their strong backs and sharp minds. Thank you to all who lent their furniture to this project and let me go to town on it, and to those who opened their homes to me for photography. Special thanks to The Paint Depot in Toronto for their excellent advice, their cheerful enthusiasm and their patience. Thanks to designer Linda Gustafson for gleefully knocking heads with me to get it all on paper, and to my editors, Sarah Swartz and Dan Liebman. My appreciation to all the people who work behind the scenes producing and printing this book and to the staff at Firefly Books.

CONTENTS

Introduction
■ 8 ■

Tools and Materials
■ 14 ■

Painting Basics
■ 34 ■

Projects

■ 50 ■

INTRODUCTION

The exciting textural techniques developed for this book are complemented by additions of metallic highlights, glorious color and arresting ideas for ornamentation, including dried leaves and vines, baskets, cutlery, beads and medallions. Any piece of furniture, old or new, and no matter the finish, can be textured and adorned to achieve a stunningly original result. Texturing can be three-dimensional, using both traditional and modern materials such as mosaic, stucco, gels, silicone caulk, or molded plaster. Also highly effective are paint treatments — such as dragging, sponging or smooshing — where layers are either applied or lifted with combs, sponges or crumpled plastic to create depth and a textured look. These treatments are often used to provide a background over which additional effects, such as stenciling or block printing, are rendered. Painted faux granite and marble, which give a *trompe l'oiel* appearance of stone, are other valid techniques. Whatever effect you seek, the textures, color treatments and ornamentation in this book will help you create beautiful works that are both fantastic and functional.

A Brush with Destiny

Many a furniture painter sets out with the simple intention of slapping a fresh coat of paint over a time-worn piece of furniture, only to have inspiration strike. The surprise result is a beautifully hand-painted work of art, a family heirloom to be cherished for generations. The flat planes of furniture – tabletops, drawer fronts and the like – present endless opportunities for decorative and pictorial techniques, while the three-dimensional form is sculptural in nature, offering many angles for viewing. Painting and decorating furniture is creativity in the round. Often the busy grain of wood, an unsuitable finish, or simply the familiarity of a piece of furniture can obscure these qualities until you stand before it, paint and brush in hand.

If you feel indecision creeping up as you try to decide on the right treatment, determine which type of decorator you are.

If you prefer furniture to be outstanding without standing out, think in terms of soft pastels or neutral colors and understated, tone-on-tone textures and treatments.

If you embrace the attitude that anything worth doing is worth overdoing, consider bright color, over-the-top decorative embellishments and a mixture of treatments for serendipitous results.

It's no longer necessary to use slow-drying oil-based paints to achieve professional results.

Using This Book

Whether you are new to texturing and ornament, or are highly skilled in these crafts, this book will show you clearly and concisely everything you need to know. Beginners are shown the basics of applying paint and choosing and applying ornament, while the advanced crafter will revel in innovative, never-before-seen ideas and application techniques. This book is more than a simple instructional guide. We have compiled a wealth of information to lead you through the maze of paints and tools available and show you how to manipulate and combine materials and techniques for wonderfully creative results. Check the *Tools and Materials* section (page 14), to acquaint yourself with the many easy-to-find and easy-to-use materials available at paint, craft and art supply stores. Unless absolutely unavoidable, only low-toxicity, water-based products are used and recommended. Water-based paints have evolved into easy-clean-up, simple-to-use, durable products.

Painting basics such as brush painting, roller painting, spray painting, staining wood and varnishing are covered, as is performing a basic paint job for those who simply wish to paint their furniture a solid color. You'll

Reading through the instructions before starting a project is like examining a road map. It helps you anticipate what's around the corner.

The toy penguin who appears in the Before pictures is there to provide scale, and is 9 inches (22.5 cm) tall.

also be referred by your project instructions to these sections as required. They provide a goldmine of basic, common-sense advice and time-saving tips.

To choose a treatment for your piece, flip through the book to find ideas that appeal to you, keeping in mind that the finished look should complement your furniture and that the projects are in a progressive order of complexity, starting with the simplest and becoming more involved as you go through the book. These advanced projects are not necessarily more difficult; they may simply require more steps, drying times or tools.

Measurements are listed in imperial units, with metric conversions following them. To make the instructions less cumbersome, the conversions are often rounded. A quart-sized can of paint is listed as a litre, for example; a yard is converted to a metre. The projects work whether you use the imperial or the metric measurements. Finally, don't let the toy penguin who appears in the *Before* pictures throw you. This little fellow is working for scale, providing a point of reference. Without him, the size of a cabinet or some other piece of furniture could be hard to judge from the photo.

Test all moving parts of the furniture.

Choosing Your Furniture

Perhaps Aunt Flossie left you a four-legged monster. It's probably a sturdy, well-built, solid piece of furniture – better quality than you can purchase today. And it's free. Instead of relegating the monster to landfill, transform it to suit your decor and get ten or possibly a hundred years of use from it. If you don't have an Aunt Flossie, garage sales and flea markets are often treasure troves of old furniture. Another possibility is unpainted furniture – especially the knockdown variety, which is ideal for painting or staining in multiple colors. And don't throw out that plastic laminate furniture. Even recently manufactured melamine-over-chipboard furniture can be transformed with specialty melamine paints.

Just as the world is divided into cat lovers and dog lovers, it is also divided into furniture painters and furniture refinishers. Refinishers feel that wood and its grain are sacred, and that every stick should be stripped and refinished. Painters, meanwhile, believe that wood is simply nature's plastic, to be transformed into painted masterpieces. The truth is somewhere in between, and this book should help balance

Interesting lines and curves can be accentuated to advantage in refinishing.

A piece with simple lines can be kept in character or transformed by texture. The choice is yours.

Elaborately constructed furniture begs for a variety of treatments to highlight moldings and other features.

the two points of view. Virtually any style, type and finish of furniture can be painted, including wood, metal, melamine and all previously painted, lacquered and varnished pieces. But please: don't paint over genuine antiques or other pieces that have historic or architectural integrity, including classics from as recently as the 1960s and 70s. If you suspect your furniture has value, have it appraised. Often, you can simply take or send a snapshot to an appraiser or an auction house. If it turns out that you own a classic, but the style is unappealing to you, sell the item rather than paint it. Antiques with original paint should be left intact. Original paint on an antique, no matter how worn, adds to its authenticity and value.

If you wish to cut down on preparation time, look for a well-proportioned piece that is solid and has a stable finish. Beware of furniture with worm holes, especially if you see sawdust on the floor around the piece – a sure sign of bugs. When they move in, these boring guests will literally eat you out of house and home. And while you can't expect perfection – the furniture is *supposed* to be old and worn – try out all moving parts to determine the aggravation factor of drawers that bind or doors that stick, especially if the vendor has them taped shut. Remove drawers to check that dovetailing is intact and that the bottoms don't sag. If chairs or tables have wobbly legs, check that they can be fixed. Bypass the item if the legs have already had surgery but are wobbling a second time.

If you are planning to apply a smooth high-gloss treatment, choose a piece with a solid, even finish in good condition. Try the

Many new pieces, like this poorly finished jam cupboard, can benefit from refinishing.

fingernail test. Scratching with your fingernail should not lift the finish. Pieces with dents, scratches, cigarette burns and water or other surface damage require a busy-looking, low-luster finish to distract from the imperfections. You may wish to steer clear of pieces with water damage that has lifted veneer. Loose or raised veneer must be removed and the scars repaired, a job that requires some skill. And take a tape measure to be sure the piece fits its final destination and can be maneuvered through doors and up stairwells.

When choosing a treatment, look for finishes that will enhance the intrinsic style and accentuate the lines of the piece.

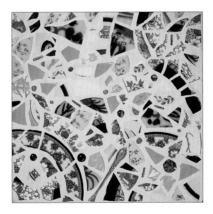

It is said that good design is form following function, and that real style is the appreciation of simple things. The art of decorating furniture captures both elusive qualities.

Choose a finish in harmony with the mood of the furniture: rustic finishes for simple planklike constructions, Victorian treatments for decorative pieces, and glossy subdued finishes for simple modern furniture.

Tools
And Materials

This section explains the properties and functions of the tools and materials used most frequently on furniture, from basecoat through decorative finishes. The ornaments and related materials needed for a particular application are discussed in the project in which they are required; for example, information on decorating with old cutlery is covered in *Art Attack,* beginning on page 86. If several years have gone by since your last excursion to purchase paint, you are in for a pleasant surprise. Advancements in the technology of water-based paint have led to long-wearing products with low odor, smooth texture, a huge color range, dense coverage and fast drying times. Brushes, rollers, sandpapers and many other tools and materials for applying these paints have been redesigned to keep pace. And alongside the paints and brushes, you'll find innovative supplies, kits and other materials for a huge range of treatments.

Adhesives

STICKY SITUATIONS CALL FOR GENTLE TAPES, SUPERTACKY GLUES AND DEPENDABLE PASTES

GLUE White carpenter's glue dries clear and is extremely strong. Use white carpenter's glue for bonding wood when joining or repairing pieces of wooden or painted furniture. Apply a generous amount to the join and connect the two pieces. (If repairing a piece, first clean out the join with a utility knife or sandpaper before gluing.) Wipe away excess glue and clamp the pieces tightly overnight, cushioning the clamps if necessary to prevent them from denting the furniture. If clamps aren't available, bungy cords can often be tightly wrapped around the pieces. When staining a piece of furniture, stain pieces before gluing, since the glue can act as a sealer on the wood, resisting the stain.

HOT GLUE With its fast drying time and good holding ability, a hot-glue gun is ideal for tacking decorative crafts. On furniture, it can be used for adding decorative detail or for finishing, but is not strong enough for gluing structural pieces of furniture. *When using a hot-glue gun, be careful.* This glue sticks to skin and can produce nasty burns. Some glue guns do produce a lower heat, but also a weaker tack.

MUCILAGE Mucilage is the amber-colored glue used in grade school. It comes in a slim bottle with a rubber nipple on top. Mucilage is the inexpensive magic ingredient used for creating crackled paint – the type that looks like flaking paint. The mucilage is painted onto a dry base coat of paint. While the glue is still wet, another color of paint is brushed over the glue. The different drying times of the glue and paint create the technique called crackle, which works best with latex paint.

TAPE Isolating areas to be painted by taping around them is called "masking." Ironically, masking tape is not a good choice of tape for this purpose. Easy-release tape, available in a light and medium tackiness, has two major benefits over masking tape. Easy-release tape is smooth and gives a crisp edge; masking tape tends to be slightly crinkly, permitting paint to ooze under its edge. Easy-release tape peels off most surfaces without disturbing the underlying finish, while masking tape often lifts paint. The only drawback of easy-release tape is its tendency to live up to its name by spontaneously falling off. The trick is to use small pieces of masking tape to tack the ends in place. Remove all tape as soon as possible after painting, preferably as soon as paint is dry to the touch. Any tape left on for long periods will leave gummy deposits or will fuse to underlying paint, tearing it off when the tape is removed.

(1) easy-release painter's tape; (2) masking tape; (3) white carpenter's glue; (4) mucilage; (5) C-clamps; (6) hot-glue gun; (7) cellulose wallpaper paste.

WALLPAPER PASTE Clear-drying, easy-to-work-with water-based wallpaper paste is the adhesive of choice for mounting large flexible materials, such as paper and fabric, to furniture. Purchase cellulose-based paste in dry form from your paint store and mix the required amount with water. This paste needs to sit for fifteen minutes or more after mixing (stir occasionally) for the granules to dissolve. Begin using the paste when it is a glutinous consistency. Use a large soft brush or a sponge to coat large pieces of paper or fabric, and use your hands to coat smaller surfaces such as découpage cut-outs and leaves. Wet pasted paper often develops wrinkles. These will shrink and disappear as the paste dries. Paper can also stretch and will then require trimming when it has dried.

SPRAY GLUE Available at hardware, paint, office supply, craft and art supply stores, this relatively new product is versatile and fast and offers a choice of temporary or permanent bond. Apply spray glue to the backs of stencils to make a light, long-lasting tack for holding the stencil in position. Spray glue can be used as a permanent adhesive for mounting fabric and posters, although it allows only one attempt at positioning. If this prospect causes anxiety, use wallpaper paste. In upholstery work, use spray glue for laminating foam to plywood, and batting to foam. Spray glue is also used for gluing block prints to a roller for continuous-printing jobs. The down side of spray glue? The overspray you get, and the amount of glue that sticks to your fingers.

When using spray glue, be careful to avoid becoming stuck on your project. This glue is tenacious. It sticks like, well, glue!

Deglossing Agents

NEW SANDPAPERS AND SANDPAPER SUBSTITUTES MAKE DEGLOSSING QUICKER AND CLEANER THAN EVER

COMPOUNDS Furniture with a lustrous finish must be deglossed before being painted, to ensure that the paint will adhere to the surface of the furniture. Very high-gloss or melamine finishes require a light sanding, but furniture that has a stable, non-flaking, low- or medium-luster finish can be deglossed with liquid deglossing agents. TSP or another liquid sandpaper can be used to dull the gloss and remove all grease and dirt. Mix the TSP with water according to the package label. Then, wearing rubber gloves, wash the piece with the solution and rinse well with clean water. Allow to dry overnight before painting.

SANDPAPER To promote the best adhesion possible between the furniture's surface and the primer or paint, lightly sand surface areas that will be getting a lot of wear, using fine sandpaper (220 grade). High-gloss or plastic laminate finishes must be lightly sanded. This is a fast job. Remember, you're only deglossing the surface, not sanding down to bare wood. Sand the surface evenly until it has a dull surface texture. When sanding raw wood, always sand *with* the grain. Sanding lightly across the grain can leave deep permanent scratches. Sanding between coats of paint with fine sandpaper (220 grade or finer) will give a smoother, lacquerlike

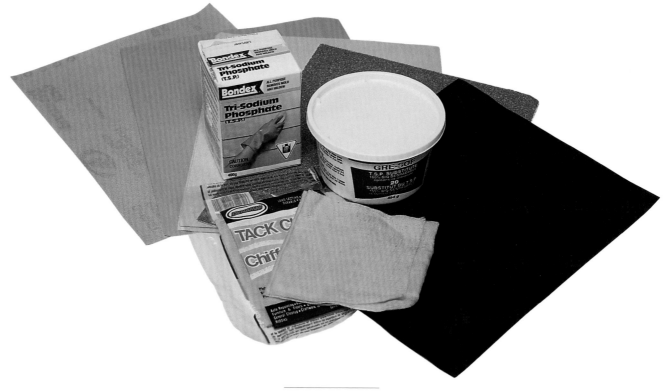

top coat. When varnishing, sand lightly with fine sandpaper (220 grade or finer) between coats. Don't be alarmed by the cloudy effect the sanding has on the varnish. The next coat will be smooth and clear. After sanding any surface, wipe away every trace of dust with a tack cloth.

Choose the right sandpaper for the job. The grit or grade, printed on the back, indicates grains of sand to the inch. The lower the number, the coarser the texture.

EMERY CLOTH Emery cloth – black sandpaper with cloth backing, and gray-black sandpaper with green paper backing – is produced only in very fine grades. Both varieties can be used wet for sanding metal or dry for wood and metal.

GARNET PAPER Brown in color, garnet paper is the most commonly used sandpaper. Use garnet paper for sanding wood, painted surfaces or plastic laminates. Available in very coarse to very fine grades, it is ideal for virtually all sanding requirements, except for sanding metal.

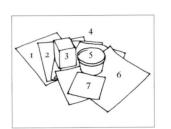

(1) fine garnet paper;
(2) sandpaper for latex paint;
(3) TSP deglossing compound;
(4) coarse garnet paper;
(5) biodegradable deglossing compound; (6) emery cloth;
(7) tack cloth.

GREEN SANDPAPER Recently developed for use on latex paints and varnishes, green sandpaper won't gum up like other sandpapers do. It is available in fine to coarse grades.

TACK CLOTH A tack cloth looks like a slice of cheese in a plastic bag. Usually it comes with no instructions, one of the mystery materials sold at hardware and paint stores. Tack cloths are an absolute necessity for furniture painting and decorating. Composed of cheesecloth impregnated with a tacky substance, its purpose is to pick up all traces of dust. These cloths work so effectively, you may want them for dusting around the house.

Vacuum up any large quantities of dust. Then, remove the tack cloth from the package, but don't unfold. Instead, use the outside surfaces for wiping, until they are completely caked with dust. Then fold the tack cloth inside out and keep wiping. Continue wiping and refolding the cloth until it is completely used. Between uses, keep the cloth tightly packed in plastic so that it doesn't dry out.

You hate sanding, so why not just skip it?
No one will know. Right?

Manual and Power Tools

TOOLS PLUS COMMON-SENSE PROTECTION
EQUAL PROFESSIONAL RESULTS

MANUAL TOOLS If you are putting together a basic toolbox, the following tools are recommended. Start with a screwdriver, the type that stores several interchangeable bits in the handle. (Some of these have a ratcheting device that saves time, energy and wrist fatigue.) Next are the screws. Old furniture that has been repaired will often have mismatched screws, and no two pieces of new furniture seem to use the same type of screw. In a perfect world, there would be one type of screw, and it would be a Robertson – the square-slot type that stays on the screwdriver. A small hammer is handy for attaching wood trim and hammering in loose nails. Small- and medium-sized C-clamps, for clamping glued pieces, are a good toolbox staple. So are small and large paint scrapers for scraping loose finish, spreading adhesive and lifting stripped paint. A small, lightweight, fine-toothed hand saw is often needed for cutting various wood trims. A staple gun is also useful. Choose one that takes ⅜ in. (1 cm) staples. If you have a lot of stapling to do, consider a power stapler. (See Power Tools, below.) Acquire additional tools as you need them. Reduce frustration by storing tools in a toolbox that keeps them visible or has shallow drawers, as opposed

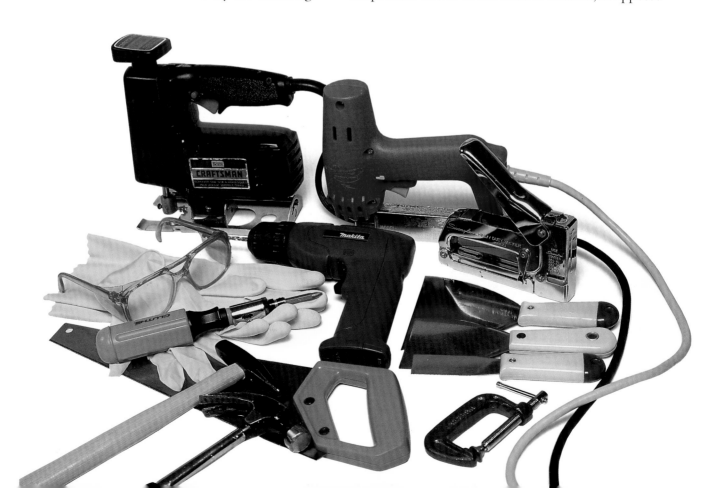

to the type with one deep box where tools become buried and difficult to find. There's a catch, however. For the toolbox to be effective, you have to put the tools back in when you're through.

POWER TOOLS

Very few power tools are required for furniture painting and refinishing. A small vibrating sander can be a handy substitute for manual sanding. Occasionally, a power drill will be required for drilling holes for hardware and leader-holes for screws. A cordless, light-weight drill with a keyless chuck is preferable. Purchase the appropriate drill bits for whatever you are drilling, wood or metal, and in the required size. A drill can also take the elbow grease out of screwing in screws. You'll need screwdriver drill bits to fit your drill. To cut plywood for tabletops or chair seats, use the appropriate saw: a table saw for straight cuts, and a jigsaw or scroll saw for curved cuts. No need to skip a project because you don't have a power saw. Many lumber-yards will custom cut wood. If cutting metal, use a specialty blade. *When cutting with any type of saw, wear the necessary protective gear and watch those fingers.* If you have a big stapling job, such as a set of six chair cushions, consider springing for a power stapler.

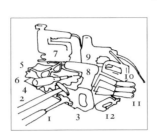

(1) 9 oz. hammer; (2) tacking hammer; (3) hand saw; (4) screwdriver; (5) safety goggles; (6) rubber gloves; (7) jigsaw (scroll saw); (8) power drill; (9) power stapler; (10) manual stapler; (11) paint scrapers; (12) C-clamp.

Unlike hand-held staplers, most power staplers take all staple sizes. The ease of operation makes the job breathtakingly fast.

PROTECTIVE GEAR

Always wear safety goggles when cutting metal, smashing tile for mosaic, or tackling any other task that can produce flying debris. When sanding, spray painting or using other materials that can produce airborne particles of paint or dust that could be inhaled, wear a paper mask that filters particles. To block both particles and fumes (or only fumes), wear a charcoal mask. For some jobs, like applying paint stripper or other toxic materials where the symbol of a hand turning into a skeleton appears on the label, gloves are an absolute necessity. Choose the heavy rubber kitchen-style gloves for these jobs. Gloves are not a necessity for most paint jobs, but many painters won't paint without them.

Latex gloves – the ones that are disposable, stretchy, lightweight and thin – are perfect for painting. Wear these gloves for jobs that can irritate your hands, such as sanding, painting, rolling paint, or tiling. No more farmer's hands and wrecked manicures. If you develop a rash or hayfever-like symptoms, discontinue wearing latex gloves. You may have an allergy.

Buying tools needn't break the bank. Buy only what you need for each job, and consider renting one-job-only tools such as tile cutters or power saws.

Metallics

ANTIQUED AND PATINATED METALLICS ADD RADIANCE

METALLIC LEAF The rich patina of gold leafing is no longer the exclusive domain of the highly trained sign painter or the refinishing specialist. Imitation gold and other metallic leaf, and the necessary components of adhesive and sealer, are available at art supply and craft stores. For genuine gold, try a framing supplier. Purchase compatible products all made by the same manufacturer. Incompatible products can cause chemical reactions that ruin the finish.

Applying metallic leaf is straightforward and simple, and the results are professional looking. The adhesive is applied to the surface area and allowed to cure for several minutes. It remains extremely tacky. The metallic leaf is laid over the adhesive and burnished to make contact with it. Excess leaf is brushed away with a small paint brush. Then the leaf is protected with a coat of sealer. Leafing is available in gold, silver, pewter and copper, all of which can be antiqued or left bright. To antique the leafing, purchase antiquing paint or use artist's acrylics. (See *Sterling Qualities,* page 92, step 3; *Mineral Rights,* page 68, step 3.)

METALLIC PAINT

As an alternative to metallic leaf, paint-on metal (made from ground ore suspended in a liquid medium), available at art supply stores, provides a dense, convincing metallic finish. Don't confuse these paints with small jars of gold and silver hobby-type enamels. You'll know the right ones if they are displayed with the compatible patinas, sealer and etching fluid. Choose instant iron, gold, copper or bronze. The labels on the jars of paint include instructions for using each product. A clear sealer, which acts as a primer, is brushed on first, followed by two coats of the metal. The metallic paint can be patinated or sealed as is. (See *Sterling Qualities,* page 92, step 6, for rust.)

PATINA

Patina is the thin sheen on a copper or other surface, produced by age. Patinating metallic paint gives an aged and refined quality to a piece of furniture.

These treatments are usually applied to molded or carved-looking decorative pieces such as pedestals; however, they are also effective on flat surfaces. Blue and green patinas are available for copper metallic paint, and rust is available for iron. Purchase the patinas wherever you buy the metallic paint. All the patinas are very watery. When brushed onto the

(1) liquid copper; (2) sheet copper; (3) patina blue; (4) primer-sealer; (5) etching fluid; (6) mica gel; (7) artist's acrylic paint; (8) liquid iron; (9) instant rust; (10) patina green; (11) copper leaf; (12) gold leaf; (13) sealer for leaf; (14) adhesive for leaf.

dry metallic paint, they begin their work, almost immediately oxidizing the metal. Apply sparingly, adding more coats to achieve the desired effect. Once the patina has finished the oxidizing process, usually three days, clear sealer is applied. Clear sealer can tone down the effect of the patina and kill the sheen of the metallic paint. It's a good idea first to do a test on cardboard to examine the effects of the sealer on the finish. If you don't seal the patinated metal, the treatment may transfer or be damaged by use.

SHEET COPPER

Try hobby shops as well as art supply and craft stores for finding sheet copper. This is the copper that hobbyists use for burnishing. The sheets are as thick as heavy paper and can be cut with heavy workshop or kitchen scissors. *When cutting this copper, be extremely careful.* The edges can be very sharp. Injuries are more painful and annoying than paper cuts. (Wearing a cast-off pair of leather gloves can help protect you.) The cut edges can be sanded dull with very fine sandpaper or an emery cloth. Sheet copper can be patinated with the same blue or green patina used on metallic paints. Before patinating the copper, treat it with an etching fluid, often called metal master, which is part of the metallic paint and patina family. Then follow the same steps for patinating metallic paint. (See *Art in Craft,* page 80.)

Metallics are most effective when used as an accent rather than as an all-over treatment.

Painting Tools

INGENIOUS NEW APPLICATORS COUPLED WITH TRADITIONAL TOOLS PERMIT CREATIVE TREATMENTS

BRUSHES Purchase good quality brushes. A cheap brush will shed hair on your paint job and fuzz up like a squirrel's tail, spraying paint as you work. A quality brush will hold paint better, paint cleaner lines and endure far more use and washing, returning to its original shape and condition.

For cutting-in on furniture, choose a brush about 1½ in. (4 cm) wide. For painting large, flat sections, purchase a 2 in. (5 cm) brush. Choose brushes made for water-based paint. These synthetic brushes, unlike their natural-hair counterparts, won't get bushy from contact with water. Buy brushes with fine bristles that won't leave grooves in the paint job. A brush with a diagonal cut on the bristles makes it far easier to paint the many corners and angles of a piece of furniture.

Tackle detail work with two basic artist's brushes: a medium-sized, fine-point brush, and a square-tipped brush about ½ in. (1.25 cm) wide. These don't need to be expensive. Just be sure the fine brush will hold a point and not resemble a small palm tree. Choose brushes compatible with water-based paint products.

To prolong the life of your brushes, don't allow paint to dry in the bristles. Wash brushes thoroughly with warm water and dish soap. Rinse well and wrap each brush in a paper towel to hold bristles in shape. Lay brushes flat to dry. Standing them on their handles spreads bristles, rusts the metal and rots the handle.

Standing brushes on their bristles gives them a bad perm. (For more information on painting with a brush, see *Brush Painting,* page 40.)

ROLLERS The small, flat surfaces of furniture are perfectly suited to a small roller, eliminating brushstrokes and imparting a smooth, even texture to a paint job. Rollers are available in many sizes and materials. A small, short-pile roller is ideal. Foam rollers can hold air, creating bubbles in the paint job. (New "velvet" foam rollers have tiny hairs that pierce the air bubbles as you paint.) Bargain or high-pile roller sleeves can also make air bubbles. These can be eliminated (along with lint from the roller) by dampening the roller sleeve and rubbing it as dry as possible on a paper towel before slipping it on the handle. Choose a tray to fit the roller. A tray provides a reservoir of paint and a ramp to roll out the excess, preventing runs, sags and uneven application.

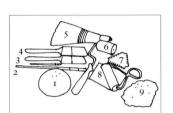

(1) synthetic sponge; (2) square-tipped artist's brush; (3) fine-point artist's brush; (4) brushes for latex paint; (5) broom for texturing paint; (6) small roller; (7) combing tool; (8) wood-graining tool; (9) natural sponge.

Roller sleeves can be washed with soap and water, but most lose their soft texture. Save them for applying primer, not the finished paint job. (For information on painting with a roller, see *Roller Painting*, page 42.)

SPONGES Sponging paint onto a surface has become the staple texturing technique for all levels of painters. Sponges, both synthetic and natural, produced especially for use with paint, are available at paint, craft and art supply stores. Synthetic sponges are formed into a half-sphere shape and have consistent, small pores. Sea sponges have large, erratically spaced pores and are irregular in size and shape. Sponging onto furniture is unlike sponging onto a full wall. Large prints produced by a sea sponge, pleasing on a wall, look crude on a piece of furniture. The scale makes the difference. Either a synthetic or a sea sponge can be used, but try to get a sea sponge with small pores. When sponging, tear off a section about the size of a tennis ball. Holding it between your fingers and making a pouncing motion, sponge sections, layering and blending colors for a suedelike effect.

TEXTURING MATERIALS The creative painter can achieve many unique textures simply by layering paint and etching it with unexpected household items. Most texturing treatments lift a wet top coat of paint from a dry base coat with a texturing tool such as a crumpled plastic bag (smooshing), an inexpensive feather duster, or a twisted rag (ragging), or by dragging a brush through the wet paint (dragging). Shadowing is created by taping and painting stripes in two finishes – matte and glossy – in the same shade. Paint stores sell many texturing devices, including textured rollers for creating wood grain prints and combs for making even-textured stripes and basketweaves.

BLOCK PRINTS Block printing is an effective method of creating multiple images for both the accomplished artist and the artistically challenged. You can purchase precut block prints made of foam, or you can hand cut your own prints. Purchase the thin, flexible foam used for children's cut-out crafts, or use a foam insole. After cutting out the block print, score details into the foam. These will hold more paint and print darker, giving the print added interest. Block printing can be done singly, or several identical prints can be laminated to a roller for continuous printing. Apply glazes, acrylic paint or latex paint onto the foam block (or laminated roller) and impress it onto the surface of the furniture, applying even pressure. Then lift it off. Potato printing is a form of block printing using a carved potato. Potato prints produce a naive, weathered print in keeping with many rustic and antiquing treatments.

Paint Products

FAST-DRYING, LOW-ODOR, EASY-CLEAN-UP PAINTS, ADDITIVES AND VARNISHES ADD TO THE PLEASURE OF PAINTING

LATEX WALL PAINT Although the experts at the hardware store may insist you need oil-based paint, just keep in mind that they're probably not computer geniuses either. Times have changed. It is no longer necessary to endure the noxious fumes, glacial drying times and tedious clean-up of oil-based paints. The technology of water-based paint products means long-wearing paint in finishes from flat matte to high gloss; low odor; very fast drying and recoating times; and easy soap-and-water clean-up.

Whether you purchase a can of acrylic paint (plastic emulsion) or latex paint (synthetic rubber emulsion) at the paint store – both types are popularly referred to as latex – expect to apply two coats for solid coverage. Don't be alarmed that the paint is a light color in the can. It will dry darker. Choose a low-luster to glossy finish for furniture. Avoid flat finishes, which show fingerprints and scuff marks. Any water-based paint should be well stirred or shaken before using. Latex paint dries quickly to the touch – usually an hour – but it should be allowed to dry several hours before recoating. Consult the label for precise drying times. Water-based paints remain vulnerable and need to cure for at least thirty days before being washed or subjected to wear and tear.

ACRYLIC WALL PAINT

This paint can be bought by the can at paint stores. Because it is water based, it is generally (but improperly) referred to as latex. Check the label for the actual contents. More expensive than latex paint, pure acrylic wall paint is considered the highest quality of most paint lines. But the reality is that when it dries, it has a rubbery finish that tends to stick to objects that come in contact with the surface for any length of time, lifting the paint (a problem on furniture). A better bet is a combination of acrylic and latex. You'll get the best qualities of both types of paint. Like latex paint, acrylic needs to cure for thirty days.

ARTIST'S ACRYLICS

Originally intended as an alternative to artist's oils, acrylic paint has developed as a versatile medium in its own right. Available in a huge range of premixed colors and incredibly fast drying, their compatibility with latex paint makes artist's acrylics ideal for creative furniture treatments. Artist's acrylics can be used straight from the tube for an oil-paint texture or thinned with water for watercolor washes and glazes. They can also be used for stenciling, freehand painting or texturing. Generally sold in small pots and tubes, these acrylics offset the need to buy a large can of latex paint, which is too much paint for detail work.

MELAMINE PAINT

The popularity of plastic laminate, particleboard furniture and countertops has helped create a generation of new high-adhesion paints, referred to as melamine paints. Unlike most other paints, which lose their grip and peel,

(1) artist's acrylics in tubes; (2) artist's acrylics in pots; (3) colored glazes; (4) latex paint; (5) glaze; (6) extender; (7) shellac; (8) spray paint; (9) primer; (10) acrylic mediums; (11) varnish; (12) gel.

these cling tenaciously to plastic surfaces. Always degloss the melamine surface by sanding with fine sandpaper (220 grade or finer) before applying the paint. Melamine paints vary from store to store. If a label indicates that a primer is necessary, use an ultra-high-adhesion, white-pigmented, shellac-based primer for best results. Allow melamine paint to cure for two to four weeks before subjecting to wear and tear or washing. If melamine paint is not available, latex paint can be substituted – so long as the melamine surface has been de-glossed by sanding and a coat of ultra-high-adhesion, white-pigmented, shellac-based primer is applied first.

SPRAY PAINT

Spray paints are ideal for painting pieces of furniture with spindles or intricate molding. Spray painting imparts a dense, smooth, even coat in a range of finishes from low luster to high gloss. It also eliminates the drips, gaps and sags usually associated with brush painting.

While graffiti may have given spray painting a bad name, this art form created a demand for spray paint that has benefited the furniture refinisher with a wealth of low-odor, low-toxicity acrylic spray products in a huge range of colors. Purchase spray paint at hardware, art supply and craft stores. Also available in spray form are textured treatments such as granite and marble; paints for covering metal or rust; varnishes; and fast-drying, crystal clear lacquers. (See *Spray Painting*, page 44, for more information on the application of spray paint.) For the avid spray painter, special nozzles giving narrow to wide coverage are available at art stores that cater to the graffiti trade.

The versatile, durable quality of artist's acrylics, and their compatibility with other paints, allows creative expression on furniture.

EXTENDER Extender is added to paint to slow the drying time. Use extender when working on a painstaking technique, such as marbling, or when applying a texturing technique, such as sponging, over a large area.

Add water-based extender to latex or acrylic paint in the proportions specified on the label. Both extender and glaze can be mixed into paint at the same time. Extender is available at art supply and craft stores in smaller quantities than what you may find at paint stores.

GLAZE Glaze, a milky-looking viscous liquid, is added to paint to make the paint more transparent, while maintaining the original consistency. Add glaze for texturing and layering techniques, such as ragging, sponge painting or dragging, when you want the underlying coat to show through to a certain degree. Some painters are comfortable adding water to paint to achieve the transparency desired for sponging or similar treatments. Other texturing treatments, such as dragging, require the paint to maintain its viscosity; otherwise the paint, if too liquid, can run together and destroy the intended effect. Add water-based glaze to latex or acrylic paint in the proportions specified on the label. Both glaze and extender can be mixed into paint at the same time. Glaze is available at paint stores in larger quantities than what you may find at art supply and craft stores.

Premixed tinted glazes are available at art supply and craft stores. These are paint and glaze mixtures sold in small jars, saving you the trouble of mixing your own colored glazes. Use these glazes for small projects such as block printing, where a decorative, overlapping, sheer quality is desired.

MEDIUM AND GEL Mediums and gels are acrylic-based cousins of the glaze and extender family. They are available at art supply and craft stores in smaller quantities than what you may find at paint stores. Mediums are milky-looking viscous liquids that dry clear and are used as varnishes. They come in a variety of finishes, from flat to glossy, and many contain ultraviolet protection to help keep underlying paint from fading or otherwise breaking down under exposure to UV rays.

Heavy gels, which are malleable when wet and cementlike when dry, can be used for a textured tabletop, as shown here.

Unlike water-based varnish sold at the paint store, mediums tend to have a rubbery texture when dry, which sticks to objects that come in contact with the surface. Gels are used for thickening paint or for texturing a painting surface. They are milky when dry and are available in a variety of thicknesses, from light (like glutinous soup) to very dense (like peanut butter). Some gels have additives such as paint, sand or mica to give them color and texture. (See *Sterling Qualities,* page 92, for using gel on a tabletop.)

PRIMER/SEALER *Primer* is more than just a first layer of paint. It adheres more tenaciously than any paint, providing a painting surface that won't peel and an even skin over the surface to prevent patchiness on uneven and absorbent surfaces. Apply primer before painting or decorating, unless you are using sandpaper or staining.

Many types of primer are available. Water-based, high-adhesion primers are ideal for most furniture. Primers that are not high adhesion are good for walls, but not for furniture. If you are using a water-based primer on unpainted wooden furniture, the primer may raise the grain of the wood. If this happens, sand lightly with fine sandpaper (220 grade) when the primer is dry. Furniture with a high-gloss finish should be deglossed by washing with TSP, or by sanding before priming.

For plastic laminate finishes, degloss by sanding, then paint with a melamine paint; or use an ultra-high-adhesion, white-pigmented, shellac-based primer before painting with latex paint. These ultra-high-adhesion primers require chemical solvents for clean-up (consult the label). Or simply use a cheap disposable brush and roller sleeve. Shellac-based primer is not recommended for varnished or lacquered furniture because it can eat into the finish.

Use spray primer for furniture with spindles or intricate detail.

Sealers have two uses. First, when painting (not staining) unpainted, wooden furniture, use shellac or another sealer recommended for this purpose to seal all knots in the wood before priming or painting. Otherwise, the knot will discolor the paint. Shellac requires a chemical cleaner for brushes (consult the label). Alternatively, you could use a cheap disposable brush. Second, you'll find that clear sealers are sold with specialty treatments such as gold leaf and paint-on metallics. These are used not only as a sealer to be painted over the treatment for protection, but often also as a primer. Purchase a sealer compatible with the products being used.

Whatever type of varnish you use, always apply it with a paint brush. Rollers, especially foam rollers, leave bubbles in varnish.

VARNISH Water-based varnishes, often called urethanes, are fast drying, with low odor and easy soap-and-water clean-up. They come in a range of finishes, from low luster to glossy, and many are non-yellowing. Varnish enriches color, somewhat like wetting down your car does, and protects your paint job against cleaners, scuffing and chipping. Several coats give a rich glasslike finish. Varnish can make the use of unorthodox materials and treatments workable, stabilizing transient color and encasing fragile materials in a durable plastic coating. It is best to varnish a full piece of furniture, though varnishing only the areas that will receive wear and tear is acceptable if a non-yellowing formula is used.

Don't view varnish as the enemy. Work quickly, avoid overbrushing and apply several coats, sanding lightly between coats. (See *Varnishing*, page 48.) Oil-based varnishes can also be used. If you find that the very quick drying time of water-based varnish makes application difficult, you may prefer oil-based urethanes. They take overnight to dry and tend to impart an amber tone to the finish.

Many a paint disaster has started on the Sale shelf — a quart of paint with a gallon's worth of tint . . . paint in the wrong color or finish . . . and paint that mysteriously never dries.

Paint Removers

NOT LIKE THE OLD DAYS – GENTLE STRIPPING AGENTS AND EFFECTIVE TOOLS MAKE PAINT REMOVAL FUN (ALMOST)

PAINT STRIPPERS If the idea of paint strippers conjures up visions of vats of steaming toxic waste, it's been a while since you tried stripping paint. There are strippers that smell like citrus fruit, and some are non-toxic enough that wearing gloves is optional. Welcome as these advancements are, stripping furniture is still a messy job, especially if the piece has intricate detail or many layers of paint and varnish. A piece of furniture with either historic or design integrity is, however, worth the journey into slime. Stripping a good basic piece buried under several coats of badly applied paint is also worthwhile, because it cannot be repainted until the

many layers are removed. But you can also partially strip such a piece, allowing sections of layered color to show through. This treatment is not only interesting and attractive, but it reveals the history of the piece.

The old way of stripping was called dip and strip. The whole piece was placed in a trough of heavy-duty toxic chemical stripper. This procedure often unglued joints and had caustic effects on the underlying wood. Most strippers today are much more gentle. Choose a gel stripper, which will cling to vertical surfaces. Placing plastic wrap over the stripper can speed the curing time. Just check first that the stripper doesn't eat the plastic.

PROTECTIVE GEAR Paint stripper will destroy the finish on your floor. Do the job over several layers of paper (newspaper is fine), with a layer of plastic or, even better (since some strippers dissolve plastic), an old bedsheet on top. Decant the stripper to paint it on. Pour it into crockery, not plastic. Wear heavy rubber gloves for this job, the kitchen type. Avoid latex surgical gloves unless you are certain the stripper won't eat through them. Safety goggles are also recommended. When you brush the stripper on and scrape off loosened paint, some particles can become airborne.

TOOLS Using the proper tools will make the stripping go much faster and easier. In the first stages of the stripping, a medium-sized paint scraper is needed for lifting the bubbled, loose paint. Next, a hard plastic stripping sponge, which resembles a block of petrified spaghetti, is ideal to use along with the stripper to help lift paint. When most of the paint has been removed, use a stripping brush along with the stripping sponge. This brush resembles a barbecue-grill cleaner, with brass bristles (they won't rust) on one side and nylon bristles on the other. The nylon brush side is ideal for giving the piece a thorough rubdown. The brass bristles remove the last particles of paint and varnish from any carving and trim, and from the grain of the wood. When using scrapers and other sharp tools, remember to let the stripper do the work. Overly enthusiastic scraping can damage fine or soft wood, defeating the purpose of stripping, which is to reveal the natural, unspoiled beauty of the wood.

(1) stripping brush; (2) rubber gloves; (3) organic stripper; (4) gel stripper; (5) safety goggles; (6) paint scrapers.

Hold it! Don't strip that antique! However worn and beaten-up the furniture may be, original paint on an antique adds greatly to its authenticity and value.

Specialty Products

FROM THE INSPIRED TO THE BIZARRE, NEW PRODUCTS ARE CREATED TO FULFILL THE PAINTER'S EVERY NEED

KITS A tremendous number of kits are available for techniques such as crackle, block printing, marbling, sponging and stenciling. Many of these kits are adequate for the painter, particularly if only a small area is to be painted, eliminating the need to buy large quantities of products that will go unused. However, some of the kits are pricey and don't live up to their promises, with poor instructions and materials that just don't work. Many of these techniques are actually quite simple to perform, require readily available ingredients and are demonstrated in this book.

SPECIAL APPLICATORS Manufacturers are scrambling to keep pace with the demand for innovative paint applicators. Aside from the usual brushes and rollers, there are combs (for creating striping and basketweave effects) and raised wood-grain patterns to be rolled and dragged. Most unusual are rollers that have plastic floral shapes riveted to them, reminiscent of a 1960s-era bathing cap. These rollers are used to create texture by layering similar paint colors, thinned with glaze, with the plastic attachments producing a subtle, semiregular pattern. Various sponges, rags and texturing brushes are available too, as are foam applicators for painting edges, corners and flat areas.

SPECIALTY PAINT Fashion designers like Ralph Lauren and Laura Ashley, who have become lifestyle/interior designers, have come out with signature lines of top-quality water-based paints in painter-inspiring rich colors. These paints are created to complement the housewares that the designers also produce. Although this approach to choosing a paint color may seem excessive to some, others find it reassuring and exciting, trusting that the results will be exactly as expected and that the decor and paint will be tasteful and will harmonize perfectly. Other paint manufacturers are producing innovative paints with unlimited possibilities for application. There are very thick iridescent paints, which are applied in layers with a trowel, sanded and glazed to a glasslike sheen. There are paints with tiny flecks of suspended color, which are made to be layered with similarly toned glazes to produce wonderful depth and suspended texture. There are also a variety of spray-paint effects, including a granitelike composition that comes in kit form. There is

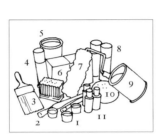

(1) stencil cream paints; (2) stencil brush; (3) texturing brushes; (4) marbling spray; (5) flecked paint; (6) marbling kit; (7) texturing roller; (8) spray granite; (9) texturing paint; (10) synthetic sponge; (11) colored glazes.

even spray-on marble veining, although it looks rather like a mix of hair and mushy spaghetti. Instead of trying to create marble veins with it, the creative painter could have fun with the effect in other unusual ways.

STENCILING MATERIALS Purchase a precut stencil from the huge selection available, or design and cut your own.

To cut your own stencils, buy stencil plastic at an art supply or craft store – the lightweight, flexible blue plastic that is semitransparent for tracing designs – and use an X-acto or a utility knife or small, pointed scissors. Lightweight cardboard can be substituted for the plastic. To execute the stencil, use any type of paint you wish: spray paint for smooth even coverage, acrylic or latex paint applied with an artist's paint brush for a freehand look with brushstrokes, or stencil cream paint applied with a stencil (stipple) brush for dense smooth coverage. The spray and acrylic paints dry quickly, while the cream paint can take as long as a week to dry. Use spray glue to provide a tacky backing on the stencil. (See *Art in Craft,* page 80.)

Don't be intimidated by the multitude of new products at the paint store. Many can add substantially to your creative pursuits.

PAINTING BASICS

Most projects in this book will refer you to this section to prepare, prime and paint your furniture with a base coat of paint. This base coat is the groundwork for your decorative treatment.

Step one is the preparation. Virtually every piece of furniture needs some preparation before painting or staining, whether you're repairing wobbly parts, removing doors, hinges and hardware, deglossing a shiny surface, or sanding raw wood.

Step two is applying the primer. Most furniture — varnished or painted wooden pieces, melamine pieces, or unpainted wooden furniture — requires priming before painting. Exceptions include unpainted wooden furniture that will be stained, and furniture to be painted and then antiqued by sanding. See brush, roller and spray painting information in this section to determine the method of application most suitable for your piece of furniture.

Step three is the painting. Paint is applied (usually two coats) over the primer in the same manner as the primer was applied. After the base coat of paint has been applied, the creative and inventive stage of adding decorative effects and treatments begins.

Skipping the preparation stage now may haunt you later.

Preparation

In the final analysis, the preparation of the furniture – fixing loose parts and preparing the surface for painting – is more important than any painting or decorating. Avoid the temptation to skip the prep stage of painting. It will yield consequences (that mom warned you about) of the same variety as building a house on sand, eating dessert before the main course, or sleeping in an unmade bed. Different varieties of furniture will require different types of preparation. Read through this section to determine how much and which types of preparation your particular piece of furniture needs. Although many painters dread this part of the job, once it is out of the way, the paint and decorative treatments can be done with a clear conscience.

Purchase new hardware if desired. If the piece has wooden knobs, consider painting them.

Right at the start, set up a comfortable, well-lit work area. Keep the work space as flexible as possible, with moveable light sources and a convenient table on which to work. You may wish to call off the bridge game and abscond with the card table. It's ideal for putting all but enormous items of furniture at a comfortable working height. Its small scale makes furniture accessible from all sides, and it can be folded up and tucked away when not needed. Keep a supply of dropsheets handy. Old large, non-slip bedsheets are good. Plastic or paper can be used, but don't use newspaper. The printer's ink will transfer to your paint job.

MATERIALS

The following tools and materials may be required.

- screwdriver
- machine oil
- new hardware and screws
- wood filler
- small paint scraper (or putty knife), wide paint scraper
- fine sandpaper (220 grade)
- sanding block
- wooden matchsticks
- white carpenter's glue
- clamps or a bungy cord
- power drill
- deglossing compound (TSP or other liquid sandpaper), rubber gloves
- tack cloth

1 *Drawers*

Remove drawers, marking their position (top, center, bottom, etc.) on the back panel. As a result of wear and tear or how they were built, drawers will often fit properly only in their original slots.

2 *Hardware*

Unscrew and remove all hardware. This includes removing doors by unscrewing hinges. On a dropleaf table, remove the hinges and the contraptions that keep the leaves up. Hinges should be cleaned and oiled. If a tabletop is removable, the painting will be easier if the top is removed and painted separately from the base.

3 *Filler*

If holes left by old hardware don't correspond to the new hardware, use wood

filler and a small paint scraper or putty knife to fill the holes. Also fill any gouges in the surface of the piece. Sand the wood filler smooth and level with the surface, using fine sandpaper.

Fill the screw holes of loose door hinges with the wooden ends of matchsticks and carpenter's glue. Allow to dry before replacing the hinges. Hinges can also be shifted when they are replaced.

4 *Fixing loose parts*

Loose desktops and dresser tops are caused by lifting the furniture by the top instead of the base. Reattach a loose dresser top by replacing the existing screws with fatter, not longer, ones. Reglue loose joins in a chair by levering the join apart, cleaning it as much as possible, then applying carpenter's glue to the join and clamping it shut. (If you don't own clamps, you can wrap tightly with a bungy cord.) Glue and clamp loose trim. Allow all glue to dry overnight.

Loose, wobbly table legs are caused by dragging the table instead of lifting it. There are many different constructions for table legs. Try to figure out how the table and legs are constructed. Glue and clamp all joins and tighten or replace all screws.

Measure and drill holes for new hardware, if needed.

5 *Preparing the finish*

Granny furniture – old, dark wood – should be given the fingernail test. Scratch the varnish with your fingernail. It should not be marked or lifted. If it is, this loose, crumbly finish will flake when painted, taking the paint with it. Scrape off the loose varnish with a wide paint scraper – a fast job. Then sand the surface smooth with fine sandpaper, either by hand or with a sanding block.

If the furniture has a high-gloss or plastic laminate finish, it will require light sanding to allow better adhesion between the paint and the furniture surface. Sand with fine sandpaper, in the direction of the grain on bare wood (sanding across the grain can create deep scratches), and lengthwise on painted pieces.

If you really hate the dust and the effort of sanding and your furniture has a medium- to low-luster finish, clean and degloss your furniture with a deglossing compound such as TSP. Mix the granules according to instructions on the label. Wearing rubber gloves, wash down all glossy areas, rinsing well with clean water. Allow the furniture to dry overnight.

Vacuum and clean the whole piece of furniture, both inside and out. Remove all remaining dust by wiping the piece with a tack cloth. If desired, wash the piece with a damp cloth and a gentle cleaner. Allow to dry overnight.

Cats seem to gravitate to the laps of those who want them least. Naturally, they're also drawn to fresh paint. Put puss out.

Priming and Painting

Applying a coat of primer before painting is a necessary step for most projects. Exceptions include furniture to be antiqued by sanding away paint to reveal bare wood, and unpainted wooden furniture to be stained. Primer adheres more tenaciously to the furniture's surface than paint does, to provide a strong bond and an even skin. The paint can then flow onto the primer without patchiness or an uneven texture.

Primer and paint should be applied by the same method. For instance, if the furniture is simple with flat surfaces, both primer and paint should be applied with brush and roller. If the furniture has intricate carving, trim, or spindles, spray primer and spray paint should be used. Don't be discouraged by the streaky, uneven quality of primer when you put it on. Apply primer swiftly and avoid the temptation to redo areas. Primer sets and dries quickly, and reworking will tear up the surface. Once the primer is dry, the furniture can be given one or two coats of water-based paint as a base coat. If your furniture has a plastic laminate finish, use melamine paint for the base coat. (See *Melamine Paint,* page 27.) Before adding other treatments, allow the coats of paint to dry for the time specified by the manufacturer.

Touching wet paint is a universal temptation, so devise strategies to keep yourself away while items are drying. Paint just before bedtime, for example. And remember, mistakes are the mother of inventive solutions.

MATERIALS

The following tools and materials may be required.

- small quantity of white shellac
- easy-release painter's tape or masking tape
- quart (litre) high-adhesion, water-based primer; or spray primer; or, for plastic laminate surfaces, if primer is suggested on the label, white-pigmented, shellac-based primer
- painting tools:
  -paint brush, 1½ in. (4 cm) wide, for water-based paint
  -roller handle, 4 in. (10 cm) wide, and short-pile sleeves
  -roller tray to fit roller
- quart (litre) eggshell or satin finish latex paint in the color of your choice
- quart (litre) non-yellowing, water-based varnish
- paste wax, buffing cloth

1 *Choosing the primer*

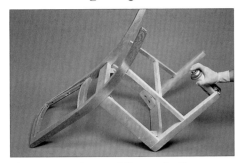

If your piece has molding, spindles or carved detail, you may wish to use spray primer. (Follow the instructions for *Spray Painting*, page 44.)

2 *Priming removable pieces*

Seal any knots on raw wood with shellac before priming.

Stir primer thoroughly before applying it. Primer should be applied to all areas that will be painted.

Start with removable pieces, such as doors or drawers. Lay doors or other flat sections on supports and mask off any sections that are to remain unpainted.

If the drawers are clean, prime only the fronts and their edges. If the drawer interiors are grungy, paint them with primer.

Use the paint brush to cut-in with primer, painting all inside joins and corners that aren't accessible to a roller. (See *Brush Painting*, page 40.) Then use a roller to prime the flat areas up to the brushwork. (See *Roller Painting*, page 42.)

The exterior sides can be primed if desired, but make sure there is enough space between chest and drawer. (Adding coats of primer and paint to the sides can cause drawers to bind.) Water-based primers and paints dry quickly. Wash brushes when they're not in use.

3 *Priming the body*

Bottoms up. Whatever the type of furniture, from chairs to hutches to tables, start priming the body of the piece of furniture from the bottom. Lay chests and cabinets on their backs and turn chairs and tables upside-down. (If the furniture is heavy, get some help lifting it.) Using a brush, cut-in all corners and places that are inaccessible with a roller. Then roller paint the primer up to the brushwork on all surfaces that you can comfortably reach. Priming the backs and interiors of cabinets, desks and dressers is optional.

Stand the piece upright. Cut-in and roller paint all remaining surfaces. Wash all paint utensils with soap and warm water. Allow the primer to dry.

4 *Painting*

Repeat steps 1 and 2, now using latex paint. Allow to dry and apply a second coat if necessary.

5 *Varnishing and finishing*

Continue, painting and decorating your piece of furniture, or if the piece is to be left a solid color, protect the paint and enrich the color by applying a non-yellowing, water-based varnish. (See *Varnishing*, page 48.)

Attach the hardware.

Binding may occur where paint comes into contact with other paint. In such areas, apply one or two heavy coats of paste wax and buff.

Paint the hardest-to-get-at areas first. There'll be less paint on the painter and more on the furniture.

Brush Painting

In spite of the numerous advances in paint tools and products, the most necessary and versatile tool is still the paint brush. But don't get caught up in brushmania. It's not necessary to buy an arsenal of expensive brushes for painting furniture. Use a medium-width brush with an angled cut to the bristles for cutting-in and for painting flat sections; an artist's square-tipped brush for narrow areas and detail work; and a fine-point artist's brush for freehand, intricate painting. While full-coverage painting is usually executed with a combi-

Creating with a brush adds individuality and personality to an otherwise straightforward paint treatment.

nation of brush and roller, sometimes brush painting is necessary to produce brushstrokes, desirable in many antiquing and rustic treatments. (See *Painting Tools,* page 24; *Specialty Products,* page 32.)

There is no foolproof way to achieve a perfect paint job with a brush. There are, however, approaches to brush painting that will garner a smoother, more even coat with fewer drips and sags. Purchasing good-quality brushes, made to be used with your type of paint, either oil- or water-based, is a good start.

MATERIALS

The following tools and materials may be required.

- quart (litre) eggshell or satin finish latex paint in the color of your choice
- paint brush, 1½ in. (4 cm) wide, for water-based paint
- tube of acrylic paint in the color of your choice
- artist's brushes, medium square-tipped or fine point
- chalk or colored pencil

1 *Brush painting a flat area*

Stir the latex paint. Dip the paint brush into the paint to a level of about one-third to one-half of the bristles. Drag one side of the bristles against the lip of the can when removing the brush from the can.

Lay the wet side of the brush on an open part of the furniture, inside an edge. Brush the paint outward, brushing the length of the area, not the width.

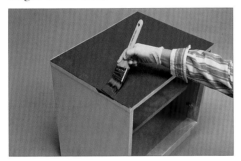

Brush toward and over edges, if possible. If the brush is dragged against an edge, as shown in the photo, the paint will form drips.

Continue brushing, quickly and deftly smoothing the paint. Reload the brush as needed. Keep a constant watch for drips, swiping them away with the brush. Water-based paint sets quickly. Avoid brushing over the same area several times.

Overbrushing will create deep brush-strokes in the setting paint. Finish painting one section of the piece at a time.

2 *Cutting-in*

When painting joins and corner detail, load a small amount of paint onto the brush and use the longer point of the brush's angled tip to coax paint into the corner, dragging the brush alongside the join. The angled cut on the brush suits this technique, especially when cutting-in on the insides of drawers and other pieces with many angles and inside corners. Watch for drips and sags, swiping them away with the brush.

3 *Painting details*

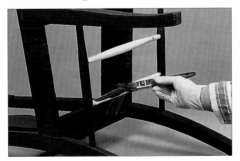

Though spray paint is usually best for spindles and other ornamental work, sometimes details must match the overall effect of a brush-painted piece. Load the brush with a small amount of paint. Holding the brush on an angle, drag it in a downward motion along the spindle, depositing the paint in a long bead.

Quickly brush out the paint to an even coat. Watch for any drips and sags, brushing them out.

4 *Freehand brushwork*

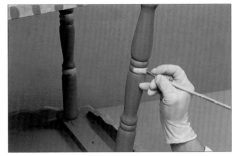

Freehand painting in contrasting colors is attractive on carved or turned details. Position at eye level the area to be painted. Use an artist's brush of a size suitable for the area, and artist's acrylics or latex paint. Thin the paint if needed so that it flows easily from the brush, but is not watery. Try to maintain a steady hand. Keep edges even and end the color at a natural break.

To paint freehand designs, such as curlicues or trailing vines, draw your design first with a piece of chalk or a colored pencil. Use a fine-point artist's brush and acrylic or latex paint, thinned if necessary to flow from the brush. Dip the point of the brush into the paint. With your hand raised (laying the heel of your hand on the table creates cramped shapes), apply pressure on the brush to obtain the thickness of the line desired. Paint the line, using the chalk line as a guide only. Following the chalk line too closely will cause hesitation, resulting in tentative lines.

Rollers are available in a wide variety of sizes. Choose one that fits the job.

Roller Painting

The roller is undoubtedly one of the most important painting tools, second only to the paint brush. It provides fast, even coverage and smooth texture without brushstrokes. A relatively recent invention, the roller has revolutionized painting. But until recently, roller painting was viewed only as a fast way to cover large areas. New, creative ways of using this versatile tool are now being explored to produce repetitive patterns and textured layering of color. For painting furniture, purchase a small roller handle with removable short-pile sleeves to fit. Buy two or

The smooth texture of a roller-painted surface provides an excellent base for creative treatments such as dragging.

more sleeves, because most are good for only one application of paint. Choose a paint tray to fit the roller. A paint tray is better than a paper plate or other disposable substitutes, because its reservoir and textured ramp provide more even distribution and better control of the paint. First, with a brush, cut-in on far corners and other hard-to-get-at places. Then use the roller to apply primer or paint, but not varnish. Varnish should always be brushed on.

MATERIALS

The following tools and materials may be required.

- quart (litre) eggshell or satin finish latex paint in the color of your choice
- roller handle, 4 in. (10 cm) wide, and short-pile sleeves to fit
- roller tray to fit roller
- fine sandpaper (220 grade or finer), tack cloth

1 *Ready to roll*

To prevent air bubbles from forming in the paint and to remove any loose roller-sleeve lint, dampen the sleeve and rub it as dry as possible with a paper towel.

Pour paint into the reservoir of the tray, filling it about half full. Dip the roller sleeve into the tray and roll it so that the full sleeve is coated in paint.

Roll excess paint from the roller on the ramp of the tray, but don't overdo it. The roller should still hold a good quantity of paint.

2 *Applying an even coat*

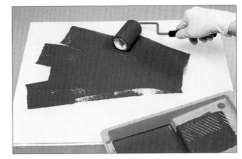

Position the roller on a surface of the furniture, inside the edges. Beginning at this central point, roll the paint outward in a triangular fashion, criss-crossing previous lines. This technique will give even texture and prevent a grid from appearing. Don't try to achieve full coverage in only one coat. Excessive paint that isn't rolled out will create stretch marks – an undesirable texture.

Apply moderate, even pressure. Let the roller do the work. It is better to reload the roller with paint than to squeeze more paint from it. Heavy pressure will create railroad tracks – a double line of heavy paint formed along the sides of the roller.

3 *Roller logic*

Roll toward and over edges, instead of pulling the roller against an edge. Rolling against an edge creates drips. As you roll, be on the lookout for drips and either swipe them with a brush or roll them out.

Continue rolling, overlapping each new roller of paint over the edge of the last, until the full surface is covered. Avoid the temptation to reroll a wet section. Water-based paint sets quickly, and rerolling will tear up the surface. Instead, allow to dry and apply another coat. For an ultrasmooth finish, lightly sand the first coat with fine sandpaper when it is completely dry and wipe clean with a tack cloth before applying the second coat. Between coats, keep paint wet by placing the tray and roller in a plastic bag, squishing the bag to eliminate air.

Block printing with a roller creates beautifully rendered, consistent, multiple prints for borders or all-over patterns. Block prints can be purchased at specialty paint and craft stores.

Be sure to check the direction of the nozzle.

Spray Painting

Spray painting gives smooth, dense coverage to furniture with ornamental carving and texture. The invasive nature of spray paint allows it to go where a brush can't reach, quickly and without drips or sags from brushing. Wherever you spray paint, large dropsheets are required to avoid home-and-garden decorating by default. Only a small portion of the paint coming from the nozzle connects with your furniture. The overspray really travels, settling on surfaces and in tiny crevices. So tape dropsheets together and cover everything that might catch drifting paint. Also make sure you work in a well-ventilated environment to avoid asphyxiating the canary. Spray painting outside is fine, unless it is too breezy. A garage with an open door is

Faux granite spray can be used on furniture if it is layered and sanded smooth, then lacquered or varnished.

best. Indoors, several open windows, or an open window with a fan, will help. Inevitably, a certain amount of fumes and spray will be inhaled, simply because of the painter's proximity to the spray can. A paper mask will screen out spray paint particles, while a charcoal mask will filter out both paint and the fumes of the paint.

Most sprays don't require primer. But if your furniture has a patchy, uneven finish, spray with primer first. Acrylic-based sprays, available in both low-luster and glossy finishes, are superb for most furniture. Choose a specialty spray paint to cover rust or to add texture. If the local paint store has a limited selection of finishes or types of spray paint, try hardware outlets or art supply or craft stores.

MATERIALS

The following tools and materials may be required.

- dropsheets
- charcoal mask or painter's mask
- one or more cans of acrylic spray paint
- one or more cans of spray primer
- one or more cans of rust-covering spray paint
- steel-wool pad

1 *Getting started*

Attention allergy sufferers: a charcoal mask to eliminate fumes is recommended. If the label indicates flammable (inflammable) or explosive, do not work where there may be open flame, including a flame as tiny as the pilot light on a stove, furnace or water heater.

Using plastic dropsheets, old bedsheets or paper (not newspaper because the ink will transfer to the painted piece), cover every surface around your furniture piece that may catch some stray spray or overspray.

Shake the can for at least two full minutes. Test by spraying paint on a piece of paper. The first few sprays may appear watery until the paint makes its way up the tube.

2 *Spray primer*

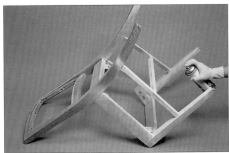

If you use a primer, apply one coat. Primer dries very fast. You should be able to turn the piece of furniture as you work, spraying all surfaces quickly. Allow to dry thoroughly.

3 *Rust-covering spray paint*

If using a special rust-covering spray paint, remove as much rust as possible from the furniture with water and a steel-wool pad. Rinse well and allow to dry. Follow the directions on the label for application and drying times.

4 *Spray painting, phase 1*

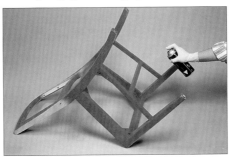

Position the piece of furniture upside-down on the dropsheet. (If the furniture is heavy, get some help lifting it.) Holding the can about 10 in. (25 cm) away from the object, depress the nozzle fully, spraying the furniture with a light, even coat. Spraying too heavily will create drips and sags. Several light coats are better than one heavy one. Spray all visible surfaces without moving the piece.

Recoat while the piece is in the same position. Check the label. The recoating instructions on most spray paints say to apply another coat within one hour. If you miss that deadline, you must wait three days to recoat. Apply as many coats as required for dense, even coverage.

5 *Spray painting, phase 2*

Allow the paint to become dry to the touch. Turn the piece of furniture upright and repeat step 4. Continue until all surfaces are covered. Allow to dry thoroughly.

The most beautiful stains can come from unexpected sources.

Staining Wood

The opaque density of paint invites creativity, but don't overlook the effect of stain on bare wood. Simple and very fast to apply, stains appear dark in their liquid form, yet are transparent when they dry. But transparent doesn't mean invisible. Stain not only provides color. As it is absorbed into the wood, it also accentuates the grain and markings. What was a bland, bare piece of pine five minutes ago is now a fascinating and intricate natural work of art. Most commercial stains for wood are nat-

Staining can be used for many purposes. Shown here, antiquing a gesso treatment.

ural brown wood shades. However, dramatic jewel tones, rustic colors or rich shades can be had from berries or fabric dyes.

After applying a commercial stain, protect the surface with wax, oil or varnish. Many stains are available already mixed with varnish or oil – making staining and finishing a one-step process. Ask at your paint store about these mixes. Always varnish natural or bright-colored stains to protect the finish and prevent transfer of color.

MATERIALS

The following tools and materials may be required.

- commercial stain in an appropriate quantity
- fine sandpaper (180 to 220 grade)
- sanding block
- tack cloth
- small quantity of white shellac or other sealer

- wooden stir stick
- paint brush
- rags
- quart (litre) non-yellowing, water-based varnish; or furniture oil or wax and buffing cloth

1 *Getting started*

Start with completely bare wood, free of paint, varnish or glue. If the wood was previously painted and stripped it must be free of all paint residue, and the surface should be lightly sanded to open the grain. Unpainted wooden furniture is often sealed – the result of saws used to cut the wood – giving the wood a slightly shiny surface. Wood that is sealed will absorb stain unevenly, giving the surface a patchy appearance. Sand unpainted furniture lightly with fine sandpaper to open the grain.

Holding the sandpaper flat in your hand or using a sanding block, sand the surface lightly with fine sandpaper in the direction of the grain. (Sanding across the grain can create deep scratches.) Wipe the surface clean with a tack cloth.

End cuts – where the wood is cut across the grain – may absorb a large quantity of stain, becoming darker than the rest of the furniture. If you don't want this effect, dilute some white shellac or other sealer to half its normal strength and brush it onto the open grain. When the sealer is dry, stain the edge.

Using a wooden stir stick, stir the stain thoroughly. Wipe the stick on a rag and double check the color of the stain on the stick.

2 *Applying stain*

Lay the surface to be stained in a horizontal position to prevent runs. (If the furniture is heavy, get help lifting it.) Dip a brush or a rag into the stain and begin to spread the stain onto the wood. Most of the stain will be absorbed.

Follow the fresh stain with a clean rag, wiping away excess. Continue staining and wiping the excess, staining to the wet edge of the previous section.

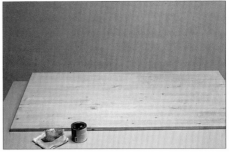

When the full side is stained, allow to dry. Then turn it over and stain the other side. Continue until all sides of the piece are stained.

3 *Protecting the finish*

The finish of a stained piece must be protected. When the stained surfaces are dry, protect them by varnishing, oiling or waxing. Consult your paint store about the different applications available.

Clear thinking: Varnish in a dust-free setting.

Varnishing

Varnishing not only protects your paint job from scuffing, chipping and the effects of cleaning compounds. It also enriches color and gives a deep, glasslike finish. Some fragile materials such as paper and fabric, when protected by several coats of varnish, can be used in unexpected and creative ways. While it's best to apply varnish over an entire piece of furniture, you may opt to varnish only the parts that receive the most wear and need the greatest protection, such as a tabletop or the drawer fronts of a dresser.

Select a non-yellowing, water-based varnish in your choice of finish, from low luster to glossy. These varnishes are fast drying, skinning over within minutes, a quality that helps prevent dust from becoming embedded in the surface. Water-based varnishes have a relatively slight odor and are easy to

Applying water-based varnish is like wrapping furniture in plastic, making delicate dried leaves tough and durable.

clean up with soap and water.

There are only two rules for achieving water-based varnish perfection. First, do it fast, quickly "floating" the varnish onto the surface with a brush, never a roller. Second, resist the urge to touch. Varnish begins to set immediately, and brush marks, fingerprints and kitty's paw prints are permanent. When the varnish is dry (usually a few hours), sand the finish lightly with fine sandpaper, wipe clean with a tack cloth and apply another coat. Don't be alarmed by the cloudy effect sanding has on the varnish. It will disappear when the next coat is applied.

Occasionally, a project with a special treatment, such as crackled varnish, will call for an oil-based varnish. These varnishes take much longer to dry than water-based ones, overnight compared with a few hours. They also lend an amber tone to the finish.

MATERIALS

The following tools and materials may be required.

- easy-release painter's tape
- tack cloth
- quart (litre) non-yellowing, water-based varnish

- paint brush, 2 in. (5 cm) wide, for water-based paint
- fine sandpaper (220 grade or finer)
- paste wax or car wax, buffing cloth

1 *Getting started*

Use easy-release painter's tape to mask around the area that you will varnish. Varnish must be stirred, never shaken. Shaking will create a multitude of bubbles that become trapped in the quickly drying varnish. While applying the varnish, stir it about every fifteen minutes.

2 *Applying varnish*

With a tack cloth, wipe the piece to be varnished, removing every particle of dust from the surface.

Using the paint brush, apply the first coat. Dip your brush to a level about halfway up the bristles.

Without wiping the excess off the brush, flow on a short, wide strip of varnish, starting near one corner or edge. Brush varnish out quickly and smoothly in the direction of the length of the surface, not

the width. Try to brush toward the edges. Brushing against edges causes runs and drips.

Repeat, brushing a second wide strip beside the first and connecting the strips. Continue until a section is complete. As you work, check for varnish that has slopped over edges and is creating drips. Wipe drips away with a brush, rag or finger. Continue across the surface, adding to the wet edge of previous strokes, until the surface is covered. Wash out the brush with soap and warm water.

Have a cup of tea and allow the varnish to dry.

3 *Additional coats*

When the varnish is thoroughly dry (usually about a couple of hours), sand the first coat lightly with fine sandpaper and wipe thoroughly with a tack cloth. The cloudy effect that the sanding has on the varnish will disappear when you apply the next coat.

Apply a second coat. Allow to dry. Sand again and apply a third coat, if desired.

Optional: Applying and buffing a coat of paste wax or car wax over the last, dry coat of varnish will produce a glowing, buttery finish.

Crackled varnish is created by layering gum Arabic over tacky oil-based varnish. The resulting cracks are highlighted by rubbed-in brown oil paint. Crackled varnish imparts a soft antiquing to painted or découpaged treatments.

A Subtle Distinction

UNDERSTATED TEXTURE POLISHES
A STREAMLINED DESK

Lacking trim, panels or other details that could draw the eye of the onlooker away from peeling veneer, this understated desk demanded a treatment to complement its clean lines, yet create visual interest with tone-on-tone texture. As textural treatments go, dragging has become a classic — and it's a surprisingly simple effect to achieve. The antiqued gold leaf adds polish and finish.

Read This First

Texturing is based on a simple principle: wet paint is lifted off a background color with any tool that will produce an even, all-over texture. A crumpled plastic bag can be used in a technique called smooshing, a twisted rag used for ragging, a comb for combing. Even a feather duster can be used to produce texture. The dragging technique shown in this project is easy and can produce wonderfully subtle results. Paint, with glaze added, is applied over a base coat of a similar tone. A brush is then dragged through the wet top coat, producing bristle marks. The degree of subtlety depends on both color choice and brush choice. Similar shades and intensities of color create the most subtle contrast. A soft brush gives finer and more subtle texture lines than a stiff one. When you first drag the paint, the texture may not be very apparent. As the paint-glaze mixture dries, the paint will shrink somewhat, creating larger gaps in the bristle lines. This technique looks best when finished with one or more coats of water-based varnish. It produces a smooth, glasslike surface and provides richness and depth to the color.

MATERIALS

- quart (litre) high-adhesion, water-based primer
- quart (litre) eggshell or satin finish latex paint for base coat, taupe
- painting tools: paint brush, small roller, roller tray
- easy-release painter's tape, 1 in. (2.5 cm) wide
- yardstick or other straight edge and pencil
- plastic for cutting triangles (grocery bags are okay), masking tape
- pint (.5 litre) glaze, paint pot
- measuring tool such as a large serving spoon
- quart (litre) eggshell or satin finish latex paint for texture, olive green
- stir stick
- small whisk brush (Softer brushes can be used for a subtle effect.)
- quart (litre) non-yellowing, water-based varnish
- *optional:* extender
- *optional:* utility knife
- *optional:* fine sandpaper (220 grade), fine brush for touch-ups
- *optional:* gold leaf and compatible sealer and adhesive
- *optional:* tube of acrylic (for antiquing gold leaf), burnt umber
- *optional:* rag or paper towel

BEFORE

A fantastic 1950s desk, solidly constructed, with simple, pleasing lines. The veneer top was loose and flaking, however, requiring extensive filling and sanding.

1 Painting the base coat

Refer to *Painting Basics* (page 34). Prepare, prime and paint the desk with two coats of taupe latex paint. Allow to dry.

2 Masking

Each section of the design for dragging must be masked. Mask a border on the desktop. Using easy-release painter's tape, tape the perimeter of the desk, matching the edge of the tape to the edge of the desk.

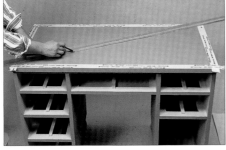

Divide the top into four triangles. Lay a yardstick or other straight edge diagonally across the desk, from one corner of tape to the opposite corner of tape, and lightly draw a line along the yardstick. Repeat, linking the other two corners.

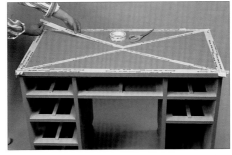

The east-west triangles will be dragged first. Use the easy-release tape to mask inside, along the lines of the north-south triangles.

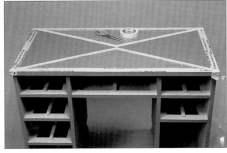

Cut plastic triangles to fit within the north-south triangles and tape them all around with masking tape, leaving no gaps. Check to be sure that no tape or plastic overlaps the east-west triangles.

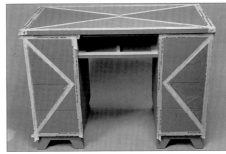

Position the drawers in their slots. Decide on a pattern for the drawer fronts. This pattern can either match or be different from the top. Tape a border around the edges of the drawers and mask around the sections to be dragged, as you did for the top.

3 Dragging the desktop

Using a large serving spoon or similar measuring tool, scoop one part glaze and four parts olive green latex paint into a paint pot. Stir well. If you want to slow the drying time of the paint, giving you more time to work, add extender.

Using a paint brush, brush the paint mixture onto one of the east-west triangles on the top of the desk. Apply the paint thickly and evenly.

Stand at the end of the desk. Gripping the whisk brush firmly, reach forward, planting the whisk just beyond the triangle. Drag the whisk straight toward you and over the edge of the desk, scoring the paint with the bristles. Wipe excess paint from the bristles. Drag a second swath, overlapping the first grooves slightly so that there are no gaps.

   Work quickly, dragging the full

triangle before the paint dries. Crooked or uneven drags can be redone easily, as long as the paint is still very wet.

Repeat with the opposite triangle. Remove the tape and plastic when the surface of the paint has set, but while the paint is still soft. Allow to dry.

4 *Dragging drawer fronts*

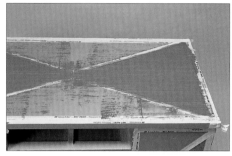

Repeat step 3 on the drawer fronts. Keep the drawers in place, to be certain the grooves in the dragging match from drawer to drawer. Laying the desk on its back can make the dragging easier. (If the desk is heavy, recruit a helper.) Allow to dry.

5 *Dragging remaining portions*

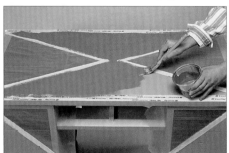

Repeat step 2, masking the east-west triangles on the dresser top and the dragged portions on the drawer fronts. Cover these areas with plastic.

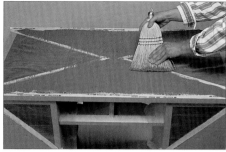

Paint the north-south triangles with the paint mixture. Drag the north-south triangles at a right angle to the east-west triangles.

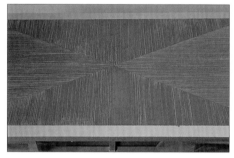

Remove the tape and plastic while the paint is still soft.

Drag the drawer fronts, dragging the remaining design section at right angles to the previous dragging. Remove the tape.

Note: If the drawers are stuck together with paint, use a utility knife (nice new, sharp blade, please) to separate them by scoring the paint where they are joined.

Lightly sand lumps and bumps smooth (where the drawers were stuck together) with fine sandpaper. Where necessary touch up with paint, using a fine brush.

6 *Gold leafing*

Optional: Gold leaf can polish and finish a textured treatment. Using the easy-release painter's tape, mask a narrow border around the dragged rectangle. Tape a square at the center, if desired. Repeat on the drawer fronts.

Using the gold leaf adhesive, paint the masked-off areas. Allow the adhesive to dry according to the instructions on the label. It will remain very tacky.

Lay a section of gold leaf onto the adhesive, burnishing it with your fingers. Tear off any large pieces of excess gilt. Repeat until all the masked areas are leafed.

Antique the gold leaf, if desired. Mix burnt umber paint with water to a thin consistency. Apply the paint over the gold leaf with a brush or rag. Before the paint dries, wipe it with a slightly moist rag or paper towel, leaving a thin film of paint on the gold leaf.

Remove the tape and paint the gold leaf with sealer.

7 *Varnishing*

Enrich the color, smooth the texture and protect your paint job by applying two or more coats of non–yellowing, water-based varnish. (See *Varnishing,* page 48.)

Attach the hardware.

Texturing in paint can refer to the visual appearance of texture, achieved by dragging, sponging, faux marble or granite (above); or texturing can be tactile, as shown in the plasterlike treatment, below.

Feat of Clay

WASHED IN STUCCO AND SEPIA, A PINE CUPBOARD TURNS CLASSIC TREASURE

Create a tiny corner of ancient Greece or Rome with faux stucco, washed in umber and sienna and enhanced by ornamental plaster garlands or seraphims. Ordinary materials and quick treatments combine for a neutral color scheme and historical mood on a dresser, cabinet or hutch.

Read This First

Choose a boxy wooden cabinet with some simple trim or molding. It should have planklike construction, rather than Victorian opulence. If applying this technique to a hutch or a dresser, be sure there is clearance around doors and drawers for them to close when coated with the faux stucco. Otherwise, limit the textured faux stucco treatment to the fronts of doors and drawers. Reserve this treatment for cabinets, dressers or hutches. The faux stucco may not stand up to the wear and tear of a tabletop.

The first stage of this treatment, the stucco effect, is accomplished with gesso, a thick white primer available at art supply and craft stores. The second stage, the antiquing, consists of brushing very liquid brown paint over the gesso, then wiping it off the high spots and allowing it to pool in the depressions. Shop for a chunky, aged-looking plaster angel or plaster fruit, often available at flower shops. Steer clear of the detailed Victorian variety sold at craft stores. A power drill is needed to attach the plaster embellishment.

BEFORE

Not well constructed and not well finished, this jam cupboard, made of pine, was serviceable but very plain. Pour on the texture.

MATERIALS

- quart (litre) gesso
- paint brushes
- easy-release painter's tape
- medium-width paint scraper
- medium sandpaper (180 grade)
- cans or other containers for support
- plaster figure or fruit
- 2 wood screws (long enough to go through the door and into the plaster figure)
- power drill
- white carpenter's glue
- tube of dark-brown acrylic paint (or substitute latex) for antiquing
- paper towel or rag
- *optional:* small wood chisel

1 Getting started

Repair and degloss your cabinet if necessary and remove hardware, drawers and doors. (See *Preparation,* page 36, in *Painting Basics.*)

The backboard was removed from this cabinet because it has a Colonial flavor.

2 Priming

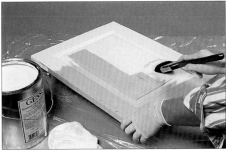

Mask off any areas that you don't want faux stuccoed. Using a paint brush, paint the cabinet overall with a thin coat of gesso. This coat of gesso will act as a primer for better adhesion of the faux stucco layer. Allow to dry. Painting the interior is optional.

3 Applying faux stucco

Stucco one section of the cabinet at a time with the gesso. Begin with the door, laid flat on cans or other supports. Using the paint scraper, scoop a blob of gesso out of the container and plop it onto the surface of the door. Move the gesso around, folding it with the flat edge of the scraper, until the gesso is in textured layers.

Different widths of paint scrapers give different textures. As you work with the gesso, it will become thicker and the texturing will become easier.

Place the cabinet so that the side you're working on is horizontal, to prevent dripping. (If your cabinet is heavy, recruit help turning it.) Do one side of the cabinet at a time, allowing it to dry before turning it to do another side. Allow the entire cabinet to dry.

4 Distressing news

Using a small chisel or the scraper, distress the cabinet by rounding off sharp edges on the trim and on corners. Be careful! Digging too deeply can produce splinters that become larger as you go on. Small chunks can easily be chipped out of the surface as well. Using medium sandpaper, smooth any rough or splintered sections.

5 Attaching the plaster figure

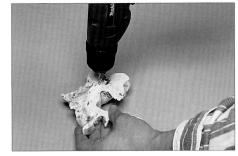

Drill two leader-holes (narrower than the screws) into the back of the plaster figure, in the thickest section of the plaster.

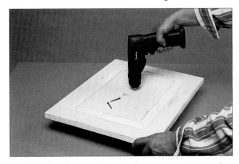

With the door right-side-up, position the plaster figure on the center panel. Check that both the door and the figure are in line (right-way-up) by verifying that hinge holes in the door and the cabinet match. Keeping the figure in position, lift it slightly and mark the position of the two predrilled leader-holes onto the door.

Remove the figure and drill leader-holes through the door.

Apply white carpenter's glue in the area of the plaster figure. Position the figure onto the glue. Attach the wood screws from the wrong side of the door, through the door and into the plaster. Do not overtighten.

6 *Antiquing*

Antique one section of the cabinet at a time. Mix dark-brown acrylic or latex paint with water to a very liquid consistency. With a paint brush, wash paint onto a small area. Allow the paint to settle for about a minute.

Using a moist (not wet) paper towel or rag, wipe across the painted area, picking up paint in the high areas and leaving the

paint in depressions and hollows. This technique will emphasize the texture. The cabinet will take on an antique sepia tone, with crevices and any exposed wood a deep brown.

7 *Finishing*

Attach the hardware and the door. Touch up any hardware with gesso and, when it has dried, antique the hardware following the technique used in step 6.

The staining used to antique the gesso-treated cabinet is a versatile antiquing effect. As in color-washing (above), paint is washed on and then rubbed off high spots, leaving crevices and nooks a darker tint. This technique works on most textured surfaces, including silicone-caulking faux plaster (below).

Heaven Sent

DIVINE CHERUBS ARE FRAMED BY GILT-EDGED DECORATIVE PLASTERWORK

Every house has room for a little opulence, a lovely departure from the ordinary, with ever-popular angel paintings in the 19th century romantic style cut into pleasing ovals of various sizes and framed with a poetic frieze of faux-plaster relief. Combined with gold-burnished sage green paint, this heavenly treatment creates a moody yet surprisingly neutral effect.

Read This First

Silicone caulking, the kind used around windows and bathtubs, is the surprising modern material used to create decorative faux plaster work. Choose paintable caulking in a silicone-based product. Silicone has the best adhesion. Buy caulking that comes in a tube with a nozzle and fits into a gun — not the little plastic packages for bathtubs. Don't be intimidated by the gun. After a few practice tries, you'll have the hang of it. Pages from an oversized color calendar of Bouguereau paintings capture the high romance of angels. For découpage pictures, select posters or calendars. These pictures are usually beautifully printed on heavy paper. The heavy paper would normally render it unsuitable for découpage, but in this instance it will be edged in silicone to disguise the cut edge. This treatment should be limited to furniture other than tabletops, where the raised decoration would topple glasses and be harmed by wear and tear.

MATERIALS

- quart (litre) high-adhesion, water-based primer
- painting tools: paint brush, small roller, roller tray
- printed calendar or poster pictures
- access to photocopier
- scissors or X-acto knife
- pencil
- tape measure or ruler
- cellulose-based wallpaper paste
- sponge, rags
- tube of *paintable* silicone caulking, caulking gun
- wire or other narrow, sharp object
- cardboard or scrap piece of wood
- yardstick or other straight edge
- quart (litre) eggshell or satin finish latex paint, in a bone or sage green shade
- inexpensive square-tipped artist's brush
- fine-point artist's brush
- tube of acrylic (or substitute latex) for antiquing, burnt umber or deep olive green
- tube of acrylic, iridescent gold
- quart (litre) non-yellowing, water-based varnish

BEFORE

A 1950s dresser with simple lines and a highly lacquered finish that has seen its share of spills and cigarette burns. To refinish or to paint? The owner decided she'd rather go decorative than understated.

1 *Priming*

Refer to *Painting Basics* (page 34). Prepare and prime the dresser, but do not paint it. If your dresser has a mirror, remove it, but don't forget to work on it at each appropriate step.

2 *Cutting oval images*

Photocopy the pattern for the oval template (page 67), reducing or enlarging the pattern to fit the top and the drawer fronts of your dresser. Cut out the center of the oval pattern and trace the oval onto the calendar (or poster) image, making four very small marks on the edge of the picture at the cross lines. Cut out the calendar images along your line.

Mark the positions for the oval pictures on the dresser by measuring and lightly marking a cross at the center point of where a picture is desired. Match the four marks on the oval to the lines of the cross.

3 *Découpage*

Following the manufacturer's instructions, mix a small bowl of the wallpaper paste. Gently rub paste onto both sides of a paper oval, covering it thoroughly. Position the oval onto the dresser.

Using a damp sponge, smooth the image from the center outward, eliminating air bubbles and wiping away excess paste. Do not rub vigorously. The printed image may rub off.

Repeat for all ovals. Allow the paste to dry. You may see small wrinkles develop in the wet paper. Summon all your willpower and do not try to eliminate wrinkles. The paper will shrink as it dries, and the wrinkles will disappear. Trying to get rid of the wrinkles will damage the paper.

4 *Planning plaster relief*

Set the hardware in place but do not attach it. Pencil plaster-relief patterns onto the dresser, avoiding the hardware. These patterns will be followed with the caulking gun.

Keep the lines simple, with large loops, avoiding intricate patterns and tight curves that can be difficult to follow with the large caulking gun. Straight lines are good for borders.

If your dresser has a mirror, mark where it sits so that the area can be avoided.

5 *Testing the caulking*

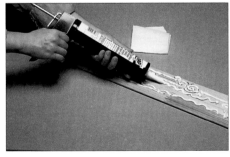

Cut off the tip of the plastic end of the caulking tube. Cut on an angle near the end, so that the hole in the tip is about ⅛ in. (3 mm) across. The tip can be recut later to a larger diameter, if desired. Insert a narrow sharp object, such as a piece of wire, into the tip and pierce the inside seal. (Some tips are removable for easy accessibility.) Load the tube of silicone caulking into the caulking gun and squeeze the trigger until caulking emerges from the tip.

On cardboard or a scrap piece of wood, do some test lines and squiggles to get a feel for the flow of the caulking. When applying caulking, drag the tip, creating contact between the caulking and the wood. No problem if you make a mistake. Scrape off the caulking while it is still damp and start again. Keep a rag handy on which to place the gun when you're pausing, since the caulking will continue to ooze.

Allow the caulking to dry. It will shrink as it dries. If the lines are too narrow and appear insignificant, recut the nozzle to a wider diameter.

6 *Caulking straight lines*

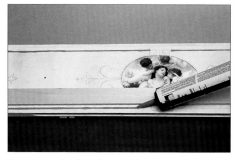

Remove the hardware from the drawer fronts. Do all straight lines first. Lay a yardstick along the line. Resting the tip of the nozzle against the dresser and the side of the nozzle against the wood, gently depress the trigger and make a line of caulking. At the end of the line, release the trigger and lift the gun off. Carefully remove the yardstick without touching the wet caulking. Let the caulking set.

The lines will not be perfect. They should be lumpy and somewhat uneven. A small point of caulking will be formed whenever the gun is lifted off, to be remedied later.

Finish caulking all straight lines.

7 *Caulking curves*

Caulking carefully around the pictures, cover the cut edge of the paper. Then, begin caulking along the curved lines. This job must be done freehand. Don't expect to follow the pencil lines exactly. They are only a guide.

As the caulking becomes dry to the touch, it is still wet inside. Using your fingers, press down any unwanted points. Allow the caulking to dry and harden.

8 *Painting*

Using a square-tipped artist's brush, paint around and over all the caulking details with the bone or sage green latex paint.

A fine-point artist's brush is useful for painting the caulking around the pictures.

Using a paint brush and a small roller, paint the rest of the dresser. Apply a second coat, if necessary, to achieve solid coverage.

9 *Antiquing*

To antique the dresser, use acrylic or latex paint in a similar yet much darker tone than the base coat. Use deep olive green for antiquing a sage green base coat, or burnt umber for a bone-colored base coat. Thin the paint to a watery consistency.

Brush the paint over a section of the caulking, working it into all details.

Allow the paint to pool in low spots. Wipe excess paint off high spots with a damp rag. Continue until all caulking has been antiqued. If desired, antique any trim or other details.

10 *Highlights*

To highlight the plaster-relief with gold, dip a brush into gold acrylic paint, wiping out the excess on a rag. Drag the brush lightly over the top ridges of the caulking, allowing paint to cling to the high areas.

Enrich color and protect the découpaged images and the paint job by varnishing the dresser with non-yellowing, water-based varnish. (See *Varnishing,* page 48.)

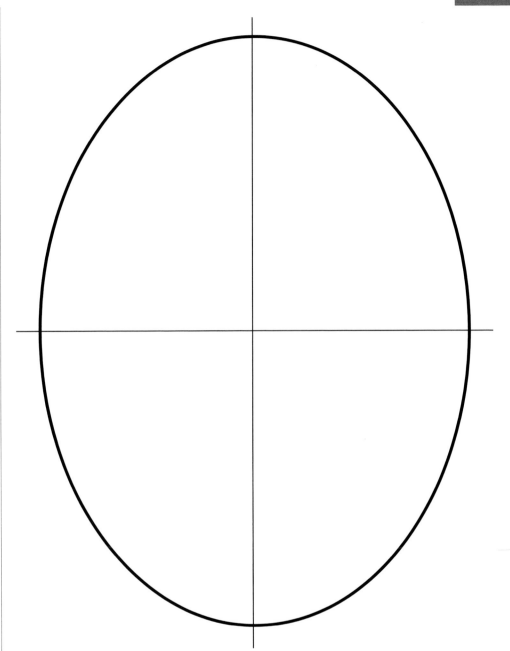

PATTERN FOR OVAL TEMPLATE

Mineral Rights

FAUX MARBLE, GRANITE AND GOLD
FORGE A MINER'S PALETTE

Gilded and polished stone, applied by the hand of an artist, is no longer
dismissed as a copy. Re-creating the aura of natural stone and ore has become an
art form unto itself. Hand-crafted faux-stone finishes should not be confused
with machine-printed melamines and other manufactured finishes. While
printed finishes are frauds, hand-rendered stone, marble, granite, or metallic
leaf treatment has a *trompe l'oiel* effect, fooling the eye for a second,
then allowing the onlooker to appreciate it for what it is —
a carefully crafted, often tongue-in-cheek replication.

Read This First

Faux-stone finishes should be executed in plausible places such as flat surfaces on bureau tops, tabletops or desktops. Some less likely surfaces are acceptable – door panels, columns, or window sills. But a complete dresser would never be made from stone – after all, it would be rather difficult to move. If you marbleize an entire dresser, chair or desk, do it with a sense of humor. In this project, first the set is painted with a base-coat color and the stone effects are applied over it. If your table has a plastic laminate finish, use melamine paint for the base coat. (See *Melamine Paint,* page 27.) The granite effect is achieved with a spray product widely available at paint stores. The normally lumpy spray is water soluble when dried and not practical for tabletops. The technique shown here, however, of sanding and varnishing the granite spray, produces a finish that is glasslike, waterproof and durable. The marbling technique can be as subtle or as bold as you wish. (Real marble comes in a staggering variety of color combinations, with veining that changes hue and intensity from piece to piece.) Antiqued gold leaf trim adds a warm and rich frame for the cooler stone treatments.

MATERIALS

- low-luster acrylic spray paint, forest green
- dropsheets
- easy-release painter's tape
- gold leaf and compatible adhesive and sealer
- inexpensive square-tipped artist's brush, ½ in. (1.25 cm) wide
- small paint brush
- rag
- *optional:* tubes of acrylics, burnt umber and/or burnt sienna

For faux granite:
- paper or plastic to cover table areas
- faux-granite spray and finishing spray lacquer (often available in kit form)
- quart (litre) non-yellowing, water-based varnish
- fine sandpaper (220 grade), tack cloth

For marbling and veining:
- pint (.5 litre) latex paint, deep green
- small quantities of acrylic or latex paint: medium-pale green, medium-dark green, off-white
- rectangular household sponge
- 2 flat plastic containers (to fit sponge)
- stir sticks or similar items
- small quantity extender and glaze (See *Extender,* page 28; *Glaze,* page 28.)
- medium- to large-sized feather
- quart (litre) non-yellowing, water-based varnish
- fine sandpaper (220 grade), tack cloth

BEFORE

A shopworn, yet interesting dining set with its elaborate table base, layers of trim and King Arthur's Court chairs. The hexagonal expanse of the tabletop is a good setting for faux stone with gold leaf accents on the trim.

1 *Painting the base coat*

Refer to *Painting Basics* (page 34). Remove the tabletop if possible. Prepare the table (and chairs), spread out dropsheets, and spray paint the edges of the tabletop. (See *Spray Painting,* page 44.)

Spray paint the table's base and the chairs. If the table has a center leaf, keep it separate from the table – but don't forget to work on it at each appropriate step. Apply two or more coats to every piece to achieve dense coverage. Allow to dry.

2 *Gold leaf*

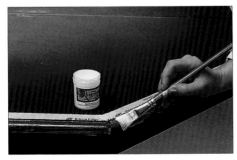

Decide which areas of trim or detail should be gilded. Using the easy-release painter's tape, mask the edges of the trim, unless the sections are easy to paint without masking (raised or isolated portions, for example). Using the inexpensive artist's brush, follow the manufacturer's

instructions and paint on the gold leaf adhesive. Allow to cure, according to instructions. The adhesive will remain highly tacky.

Remove the tape. Lay a sheet of gold leaf onto the adhesive. Burnish it with your fingers, pressing it into recessed areas with a toothpick or the point of a paint-brush handle. Tear off any large pieces of excess leaf and reserve them. Repeat until all adhesive is covered with gold leaf. Small cracks in the gold leaf are desirable.

Using a small paint brush (fairly stiff bristles are preferred), flick away all excess gold leaf – a surprisingly messy job, spreading fairy gold all over the place.

Apply gold leaf to the chairs and the table base. To apply gold leaf to finials or rungs, paint on the adhesive. Then wrap a sheet of gold leaf around, working the gilt into crevices or details. Cover any bare spots with scraps of gold leaf.

Paint sealer over all gold leaf sections and allow it to dry.

3 *Antiquing*

Optional: To make the gold richer and subdue the brightness, antique the gold leaf. Mix a small quantity of burnt umber and/or burnt sienna acrylics with water to create a watery consistency. Paint a section of gold leaf with the brown paint.

Wait for about two minutes. Wipe the section with a slightly damp rag, removing the excess. A thin film should remain, toning down the bright quality of the leaf and enriching the color. Allow the antiquing to dry. Then paint with a coat of sealer.

To make cushions for the finished chairs, see *Seating,* page 112.

4 *Faux granite*

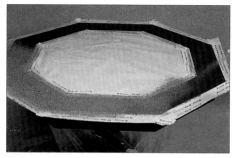

Using the easy-release painter's tape, mask off the area to receive the faux-granite treatment. Spread dropsheets and cover the rest of the table with paper or plastic taped in place. Allow no gaps.

Spray the masked-off section with the faux-granite spray, achieving a solid coverage. Allow to dry. It will be bumpy and speckly.

Use the spray lacquer that comes with the spray granite and spray the faux granite thoroughly, following the directions on the can. Allow to dry.

Paint a coat of the non-yellowing, water-based varnish onto the faux granite. Allow to dry.

Using fine sandpaper, *very lightly* sand the granite. Sanding will smooth some of the bumps. Don't be alarmed if the granite appears cloudy from the sanding. Use a tack cloth to wipe the surface completely clean of all dust. Then apply another coat of varnish. The granite should be fairly smooth. More varnish, which will give the granite a completely smooth surface, will be applied later. Allow to dry. (See *Varnishing,* page 48.)

5 *Marble base coat*

Remove all tape and paper from the tabletop, leaving the dropsheet on the table base for protection. If the table has a center leaf, place it into the table. Determine which areas will be marbled. Mask around these areas with easy-release tape. Paint the marble sections with a base coat of deep-green latex paint. Allow to dry.

6 *Marbling*

Lightly dampen the household sponge. Create a cratered moonscape – the more cratered, the better – on one side of the sponge by pulling small, irregular chunks out of the surface. Set the sponge aside.

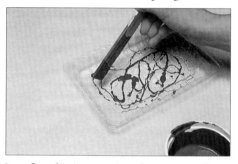

In a flat plastic container large enough to accommodate the sponge, use a stir stick or other implement to drizzle ribbons of extender and glaze in a random pattern. (See *Extender,* page 28; *Glaze,* page 28.) Then drizzle medium-pale green and, on top of that, medium-dark green. Thin the paint with water if necessary. Neither of these colors should be as dark as the deep-green base coat.

Hold the still-damp sponge flat, crater-side-down, and dip it into the drizzled paint. Don't squish it or move it in any way that will mix the paint. Lift the sponge and dip again in another section of the flat container.

Pat the paint side of the sponge onto the base coat of the tabletop, making a curved path of color. When patting, never drag the sponge. Use only an up-and-down motion. Work over the path, patting lightly outward from the center. The more patting, the more soft and graduated the color will be. Continue in this manner, creating several lighter pathways of color that gently blend into the base coat.

This process creates the softly textured-looking background colors of the rock formation. Stand back from the table and squint to see a pattern emerge. When working across the table's center leaf, try to balance the design so that, when the center leaf is removed, the pattern will match fairly closely. If the center leaf will be a fairly permanent fixture, it is more important that the design match from the table to the leaf and across it. But if it will seldom be used, concentrate on matching the design with the center leaf removed. (Ideally, the design will match both with and without the center leaf.) Remove the leaf and lightly touch up the pattern to make it match across the division.

7 Veining

Do the veining with the center leaf out of the table and the table closed. Drizzle small, equal amounts of extender, glaze and off-white paint into a flat container. Don't mix.

Take the feather and dip a length of the feathery edge into the container, allowing the feather to pick up both paint and extender.

Starting at an edge close to you, place the feather lightly onto the table and push it away from you. As you push, make your hand tremble in small jerking movements.

Don't give in to the urge to drag the feather toward you. If you do, the veining will look very regular and phony. As you progress, the edge of the feather will break up into segments, producing multiple lines in various widths, all following the same motion. This look is desirable. For best results, push the feather using the left hand (if you are right-handed), and vice versa.

For a natural appearance, remember that most veining should radiate from one point, breaking into branches that in turn create additional points of origin for more veins. Stand back regularly to see the overall pattern of the veining. Veining can be as subtle or as bold as you'd like.

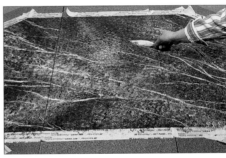

Place the center leaf into the tabletop. Join the veins from one side of the leaf to the other, using the feather and paint mixture.

8 Varnishing

To protect the paint, enrich the color and impart a deep, glasslike finish, give the tabletop, including the granite, three coats of non-yellowing, water-based varnish. Sand lightly with fine sandpaper and wipe with a tack cloth between each coat. Varnish the center leaf separately. (See *Varnishing,* page 48.)

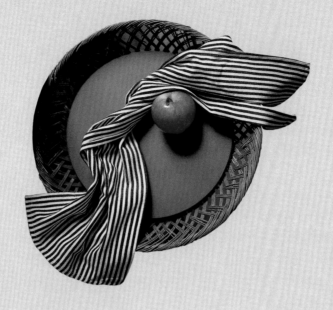

Basketry

BASKETS ADD FRIVOLITY TO TINY TABLES

The texture and color of a basket add whimsy and a whole new purpose to
the classic, simple design of a tiny lamp table. A dependable lamp table is
an ideal pedestal for a basket, especially when finished to coordinate
with the surrounding decor. Three individual approaches — color-wash in
country blue, natural cane with accents of black, and wholly natural twigs —
show the versatility of this treatment. Load the finished table with
fruit or plants, or use it as an ingenious bread basket at your
next dinner party — no table space required.

Read This First

A knockdown table or one that can be easily taken apart is needed for this project. Choose a low-profile basket with a flat bottom to add a textured rim to the table, or select a chunkier basket complete with handle to create a plant stand. When you go on your basket hunt, take the tabletop along and check that it fits, easily, *flat inside* the base of the basket. After selecting the basket, decide on a treatment and choose spray paint or a faux finish for the base and top. The base and tabletop are painted with a base coat first. Then the basket is finished to coordinate, and the table is assembled. If your table has a plastic laminate finish, use melamine paint for the base coat. (See *Melamine Paint,* page 27.)

MATERIALS

For all tables:

These materials are required for all tables. They're also all you need for making the *Natural Plant Stand* (see photo, bottom right, page 74).

- basket to fit the tabletop
- fine sandpaper (220 grade), tack cloth
- 1 can spray paint or spray faux finish (for base), in an appropriate color (step 2)
- ruler or tape measure
- utility knife, heavy-duty scissors, or garden clippers
- corrugated cardboard
- white carpenter's glue
- stapler and staples, or screws and washers
- *optional:* masking tape

For a color-washed table:

See photo, top, page 74.

- 1 pint (.5 litre) primer or gesso (available at art supply shops)
- sponge or 1½ in. (4 cm) paint brush; rag
- small quantity flat latex paint, country blue (acrylic may be substituted)

For a brush-painted table:

See photo, bottom left, page 74.

- 1 can glossy acrylic spray paint, black
- pint (.5 litre) primer
- pint (.5 litre) eggshell latex, off-white
- tubes of acrylics: yellow oxide, burnt sienna, mars black
- rag or paper towel
- fine-point artist's brush
- *optional:* 2 plastic bags and tape
- *optional:* pencil
- *optional:* spray varnish

BEFORE

These inexpensive little knockdown lamp tables are sold at discount department stores.

FOR ALL TABLES

1 Sanding

With the table still in pieces, lightly sand the top of the table with fine sandpaper. Wipe completely clean of all dust, using a tack cloth. Legs may be sanded too, if finish is glossy.

2 Spray painting

Spray paint the base of the table with two or three coats as needed, following the manufacturer's instructions.

If making a *Color-Washed Table*, spray paint the base and top of the table a country-blue shade.

If making a *Brush-Painted Table*, spray paint only the table's base with glossy black. Do not paint the top.

If making a *Natural Plant Stand*, spray paint the base and top with faux-stone or granite spray paint in beige or gray. (See *Spray Painting*, page 44.)

Optional: To prevent paint build-up that can make assembly difficult, you may wish to tape the areas of the legs that slide into the center pole before painting.

3 Cutting the basket

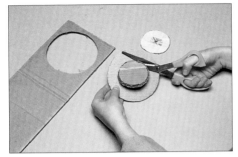

Turn the tabletop upside-down and measure the diameter of the flange (the wooden circle in the center that the base screws into).

Cut a hole in the center of the basket, matching the diameter of the flange. If the basket has a loose, delicate weave, apply masking tape across the area before cutting.

Depending on the weight of the basket, use a utility knife, heavy-duty scissors or garden clippers for the cutting.

4 Cardboard washer

Cut a circle of corrugated cardboard, 4 in. (10 cm) larger in diameter than the flange on the underside of the tabletop. Cut a hole in the center of the cardboard circle to match the hole in the basket. Spray paint the cardboard if desired. Set the cardboard aside to be used when assembling the basket and table.

5 Basket treatments

To color-wash the basket, follow the steps for a *Color-Washed Table* (page 78). To brush paint the tabletop and basket, follow the steps for a *Brush-Painted Table* (page 79).

If you wish to make a *Natural Plant Stand*, move on to the next step, number 6.

6 *Attaching basket to top*

Apply carpenter's glue to the underside of the tabletop, avoiding the center flange. Place the tabletop upside-down on a support, like a small box. Position the basket upside-down, centering it onto the tabletop, with the hole of the basket centered over the flange. The flange should show.

Place the cardboard grommet around the center flange. Staple the basket to the top. Be sure to use staples that will penetrate through the basket and into the tabletop.

If the basket is too thick for staples, use screws with washers. The washers will prevent the screws from pulling through the weave of the basket. Be certain the screws are long enough to penetrate the washer and the basket and go *partway* through the tabletop.

7 *Assembly*

Assemble the base. Then screw the base into the tabletop.

COLOR-WASHED TABLE

Choose a rustic basket with a nubby weave in a light- to medium-colored cane.

A *Getting started*

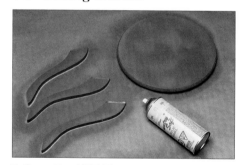

Follow *For All Tables,* steps 1 to 4.

B *White washing*

Thin the primer or gesso so that it runs easily from a brush. Using a brush, sponge or rag, prime the basket white, working it into all crevices. While working, use a damp rag to wipe the basket at random places, lifting the white in places to expose the natural cane on high spots. Allow to dry.

C *Blue washing*

Mix latex or acrylic paint to obtain a country-blue shade. Thin the paint to a soupy consistency. Work the blue paint over the basket as you did with the primer, using a brush, sponge or rag. While the paint is still wet, use a damp 08rag to lift the paint at random places from high spots, exposing both primer and natural cane. Allow to dry.

D *Finishing*

Follow *For All Tables,* steps 6 and 7.

BRUSH-PAINTED TABLE

Choose a basket with a flat weave. Inexpensive baskets of this type are readily available at stores in Chinatown. Particularly attractive are baskets with brass accents.

A *Getting started*

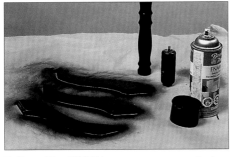

Follow *For All Tables*, steps 1 to 4, painting the base a glossy black. Do not paint the tabletop.

B *Painting the top*

Paint the tabletop with primer and two coats of off-white latex paint. Allow to dry.

Mix together the yellow oxide and burnt sienna acrylics. Thin the paint mixture with water to a watery consistency.

Dip a rag or paper towel into the paint and rub it lightly over the tabletop. This finish will be uneven and should coordinate with the basket. Allow to dry.

C *Painting the basket*

Optional: While the tabletop is drying, cut open two plastic bags. Place one over the outside of the basket, and the other on the inside. Tape the bags securely to the bottom edge of the basket's rim, leaving only the rim of the basket exposed. Spray paint the rim with two coats of glossy black. Allow to dry and remove the tape and plastic.

Using the fine-point artist's brush and mars black paint, paint freehand curlicues onto the tabletop. Thin the paint with water, if necessary, so that it flows easily from the brush. The curlicues should look hand painted, not perfect. Draw curlicues first in pencil, if desired, but don't attempt to follow your pencil lines too closely. Instead, use them only as a guide. Try to do the curlicue in one smooth motion. Add small dashes at odd angles around the curlicues. Allow to dry.

Paint a zigzag border and random dashes on the outside of the basket. Paint a zigzag border on the inside. Allow to dry.

D *Varnishing*

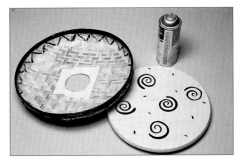

Optional: To protect the paint job, spray both sides of the basket and the tabletop with spray varnish. Allow to dry.

E *Finishing*

Follow *For All Tables*, steps 6 and 7.

Art in Craft

ATTENTION-GRABBING LAYERED COLOR IS OFFSET BY CRAFTED COPPER

Acid green, layered over brilliant blue paint and spiced with crafted and stenciled copper, renders an outdated desk a vibrant piece of contemporary art. This desk has aggressive texture, color and pattern — elements that create a novel, fast-forward piece. Not for the faint of heart, this combination of tactile materials, random stencils and vivid colors takes some nerve. But accolades from admirers will reward your daring decision.

Read This First

Acid and cool colors rub up against each other in this paint technique. The paint treatment consists of layering color, then lightly sanding the coats with a hard plastic stripping sponge to expose the underlying colors. If your desk has a plastic laminate finish, use melamine paint for the base coat. (See *Melamine Paint,* page 27.) Also demonstrated is dry brushing, a technique with an effect similar to sanded paint. The stenciling can be done in any contrasting color or in a metallic leaf – gold, copper or silver – with a purchased or homemade stencil. For metallic leaf, you'll need the compatible leaf, adhesive and sealer. For the copper cut-outs buy one or more sheets of copper, the type used for copper-burnishing kits. You will also need copper etching fluid and patina in blue or green. These chemical treatments, used to oxidize the copper and produce a patina, are available at art supply and craft stores.

MATERIALS

- quart (litre) high-adhesion, water-based primer
- eggshell finish latex paint, 1 quart (litre) each: brilliant blue, moss green, chartreuse green
- painting tools: paint brush, small roller, roller tray
- plastic paint-stripping sponge
- rag or scrap paper
- inexpensive square-tipped artist's brush, ½ in. (1.25 cm) wide
- purchased stencil, or stencil plastic or cardboard (step 4)
- spray glue; scrap paper or dropsheet
- copper leaf and compatible adhesive and sealer
- sheet of thin copper, heavy scissors
- etching fluid for copper (often called "Metal Master," and available at art supply and craft stores)
- rag or paint brush
- patina blue or green fluid (available at art supply and craft stores), soft paint brush
- sealer (made by manufacturer of the patina)
- small hammer and small brass nails
- quart (litre) non-yellowing, water-based varnish
- *optional:* needle-nosed pliers

BEFORE

Lacking personality, this mediocre desk deserves some zip.

1 *Painting*

Refer to *Painting Basics* (page 34). Prepare, prime and paint the body of the desk with two coats of brilliant blue latex paint. Paint the drawer fronts with two coats of moss green. Allow to dry.

Paint moss green over the body of the desk, brushing it on at random. Allow to dry.

Paint chartreuse in random areas over the drawer fronts. Allow to dry.

2 *Painting and distressing*

Paint one coat of chartreuse over the body of the desk, with as much coverage as possible. When the paint is dry to the touch, firmly buff it with the paint-stripping sponge, removing layers of paint and exposing the undercoats in areas where the desk would naturally show wear, such as along all trim, on corners and in random spots on the top and sides. Try not to rub through all layers to the primer. If you accidentally do, however, you can touch up areas later.

Paint the drawer fronts with the brilliant blue. Buff through the paint, exposing various layers.

3 *Dry-brush technique*

Using a dry-brush technique add more contrasting color to the surface, if desired. Dip the artist's brush into the paint. Wipe excess paint onto a rag or piece of scrap paper. Brush the remaining paint onto the desk surface. This is a lot like wiping out a used brush, leaving a thin, somewhat transparent layer of paint on the surface. The paint will be dense where you start, becoming thinner the more you brush. Make any touch-ups as required.

4 *Stenciling copper leaf*

Add stenciled copper leaf designs onto the desk in a random fashion. Use a purchased stencil, or cut a design from stencil plastic (available at craft stores) or lightweight cardboard. For ease of stenciling, coat the back of the stencil with spray glue. Allow the stencil to sit for an hour or more until the glue is lightly tacky. Lay the stencil onto the desk and paint the image area with adhesive for the copper leaf. Remove the stencil. Repeat in all locations where a stenciled pattern is desired. Allow the adhesive to set. It will remain very tacky.

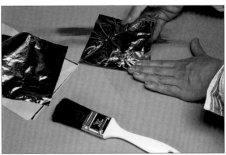

Lay a sheet of copper leaf onto the adhesive. Burnish it with your fingers.

Using a small paint brush, brush excess copper leaf from the edges of the image. Repeat for all stenciled areas of adhesive. Using the sealer for the copper leaf, paint the stenciled copper leaf designs.

5 *Sheet copper*

Draw patterns and trace them, or cut shapes freehand from the sheet copper. *When cutting this copper, be extremely careful. The edges can be very sharp. Injuries are more painful and annoying than paper cuts. (Wearing a cast-off pair of leather gloves can help protect you.)*

Lay the cut-outs right-side-up on paper and paint them with etching fluid.

Using a rag or a paint brush, coat the cut-outs with either patina blue or green. Allow to dry and to turn color. Check the instructions on the jar of sealer to determine the length of time you need to wait before sealing (often three days).

Using a dry soft paint brush, brush away excess patina.

Coat the patina side of the copper with sealer. Allow to dry.

Using a small hammer and small brass nails, nail the copper cut-outs in place on the desk. If the nails are very short, use needle-nosed pliers to hold the nails while hammering.

Protect the paint, smooth the edges of the copper pieces and enrich color by painting the desk with two or three coats of non-yellowing, water-based varnish. (See *Varnishing,* page 48.)

Attach the hardware.

*Stenciling metallic leaf on a textured ground adds richness as well as contrast.
Shown here, a moon and stars motif, in copper, on a suedelike, sponge-
painted background. Inspired hardware accentuates the effect.*

Art Attack

ADORNMENTS AND FANCIFUL PAINT CONCOCT A WORK OF ART

Putting the funk in functional, defying labels, this startling, heavily ornamented chair is at once a gypsy's suitcase of beads and baubles, a collection of folk wind chimes, a work of abstract art and a statement on the creative kitchen. Lively freehand images, painted in primary colors, mix with found pieces of beads and silver cutlery to give the ultimate makeover to a sturdy old pantry chair.

Read This First

A time-consuming but not difficult job, adorning this chair takes some paint, beads, cast-off cutlery or other adornments – and a sense of humor. Hunting the silver cutlery is part of the adventure of finishing this piece. Stainless steel simply doesn't make the grade. Find silver-plated or solid silver mismatched and damaged pieces of cutlery at a Goodwill, Salvation Army or similar type of store. These shops usually have a box of single and broken pieces for as little as a dime each. Most antique or *junque* stores charge far too much for silver to be used in this way. A jigsaw and drill with attachments for metal must be used to cut and pierce the cutlery. If you are intimidated by power tools, substitute medallions or pieces from old jewelry or clockworks that have holes for attaching. Use beads with a center hole large enough for a sewing needle. (Beading needles are slimmer, but can't be threaded with a heavy thread.) Treat this project as a creative process to be done in stages, whenever the mood strikes.

BEFORE

Chunky, sturdy and pea-soup green, this chair is suitable for a wide range of treatments, including the outrageous.

MATERIALS

- quart (litre) high-adhesion, water-based primer or can of spray primer
- latex or tubes of acrylics in various colors: mars black, tangerine, turquoise, bubble gum pink, royal blue
- paint brush, 1 in. (2.5 cm) wide
- fine-point artist's brush
- random silver cutlery or similar found objects, appropriate metal polish
- jigsaw and metal cutting blade
- power drill and small-diameter metal-drilling bit
- needle-nosed pliers
- clear spray varnish or lacquer
- small screw-eyes
- miscellaneous beads (center hole should be large enough for a sewing needle), piece of velvet
- scissors, sewing needle, button-hole thread
- *optional:* small brass nails, hammer and nail
- *optional:* clamps, rags

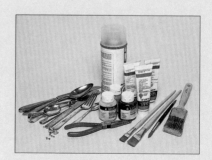

1 *Painting*

Refer to *Painting Basics* (page 34). Prepare and prime the chair. Allow to dry.

Start from the bottom of the chair. Using the 1 in. (2.5 cm) paint brush, paint sections of the chair in various colors with one or two coats of latex or acrylic paint. Wash the brush between colors.

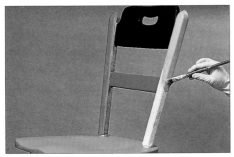

When the paint is dry, turn the chair upright and paint the top and back. Allow to dry.

2 *Freehand painting*

Using the fine-point artist's brush, paint designs onto the large surfaces of the chair, particularly the seat and the back-rest. Add stars, curlicues, stripes, etc., to other parts as desired.

For best results, thin the paint so that it flows easily from the brush point. Draw the patterns freehand and quickly to avoid bunched-up, tentative lines. Realism is not a concern. Set the painted chair aside and allow to dry.

3 *Cutting the cutlery*

Polish the cutlery.

Using a jigsaw with a metal-cutting blade, cut the ends off several pieces of the cutlery. *Wear goggles for this job, and watch your fingers.* If the pieces require clamping to secure them while cutting, pad the clamped sections with rags to prevent the clamp from leaving gouges in the silver.

Drill holes in the silver for hanging. Place the pieces on a wooden board, and drill a hole centered at one end of each piece. Use a power drill fitted with a small-diameter drill bit designed for drilling metal. *Wear goggles for this job.*

4 *Bending the cutlery*

Make the fork tines expressive by bending them into a variety of tight and loose curls in different directions. Grasp the tip of a tine in the point of a pair of needle-nosed pliers and turn it to the desired curl. If you wish, pad the pliers to prevent marks on the silver. Handles can also be bent or curled. The ease of bending will vary greatly from piece to piece. Some cutlery may be too stiff to bend.

5 *Sealing*

When you've completed all polishing, cutting, drilling and bending, spray all sides of the cutlery with a clear varnish or lacquer. This will prevent tarnishing. Allow to dry.

6 *Hanging silver and beads*

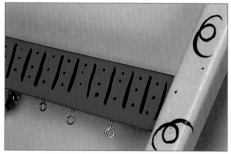

Decide on the best places to hang the cutlery and beads. Screw small screw-eyes into the chair in the locations selected. Creating a small hole with a hammer and nail can help you start the screw-eye. A nail through the screw-eye can help provide leverage to turn it.

Spreading the beads on velvet will help prevent them from rolling away. Thread a small- to medium-sized sewing needle with thread, doubled. Thread one or more beads.

Slip the needle through a screw-eye, and then back through the beads.

Slip the needle through a drilled hole in one of the pieces of silver. Tie a tight square knot in the thread. Cut the thread close to the knot. You may be able to cover the knot by sliding a bead over it.

Repeat for the remaining silver pieces, creating whatever combinations of beads and silverware you desire.

7 *Finishing touches*

Pieces of silverware can be nailed onto flat areas of the chair by hammering brass nails through the drilled holes. But be sure your placement won't be a pain in the butt.

*If cutting and manipulating cutlery seems too difficult, add a kitchen motif with
mosaic made from smashed china plates (see Mad for Mosaic, page 104),
or with découpaged food-related pictures (see Heaven Sent, page 62).*

Sterling Qualities

SILVER AND MICA PUT
FIRE INTO THE IRON

Ignore the gold rush. Silver and its cousins — iron, aluminum, pewter and

chrome — create accents with both a presence and a cool neutrality. A small

wooden end table gets a novel twist when the very convincing antiqued silver

leaf makes it look too heavy to lift. Topping this table: gel infused

with mica, scored with freehand designs and impressed with

pewter medallions and silver buttons.

Read This First

This project produces unusual and daring results. Each of the stages to completion is straightforward. It's the combination that is startling. For this treatment, choose a table that is small and has a recessed top with a lip around it, possibly one that has a missing glass insert. First you spray paint the table a deep base color. If your table has a plastic laminate finish, use melamine paint for the base coat. (See *Melamine Paint,* page 27.) Over this color, apply silver leaf. Along with the silver leaf, use the compatible adhesive and sealer made by the same manufacturer – and buy enough to do the whole base of the table.

When the silver leaf is complete and antiqued, the mica-gel top is applied to the recessed tabletop. This is a very thick gel mixed with mica, which gives it a black iridescence. Gels with other additives are also available, but buy the heaviest consistency available. The density of the gel lets you carve and embed it with medallions and coins, which enhance the tone-on-tone nature of the piece. If desired, instant iron can be added to the table center and rusted to perfection, providing an unexpected touch of rust-red. Purchase these materials at art supply and craft stores.

BEFORE

An ordinary wooden end table. At second glance: some attractive lines, and interesting scored trim that deserves highlighting.

MATERIALS

- low-luster acrylic spray paint, 1 can each of deep green and black
- silver leaf, adhesive and sealer to cover the entire base of the table (Buy compatible products.)
- paint brush, 1 in. (2.5 cm) wide
- small, stiff-bristled house-painting brush
- mica gel or other heavy-consistency colored or textured gel (enough to cover and fill the top of the table)
- narrow and wide paint scrapers
- silver medallions, silver buttons, coins, or other flat objects
- wiping cloth
- *optional:* tubes of acrylics, pthalo green and Payne's gray
- *optional:* rags or paper towels
- *optional:* instant iron, instant rust (available at art supply and craft stores); fine-point artist's brush

1 *Spray painting*

Refer to *Painting Basics* (page 34). Prepare your table (*Preparation,* page 36). Then turn to *Spray Painting* (page 44), and spray paint the table with the black and green spray paints. Spray each color in sections, overlapping the colors. These variegated colors will show through cracks in the silver leaf when it is applied, giving it a rich appearance. Allow the spray paint to dry.

2 *Silver leaf*

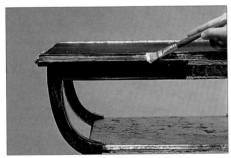

The silver leaf should be applied to the base and around the rim of the top, but not on the top (the gel will be applied there).

Following the instructions on the jar, use the 1 in. (2.5 cm) paint brush to apply the adhesive for the silver leaf to a section of the table. Allow the adhesive to cure for the time specified. The adhesive will remain very sticky.

Remove a sheet of silver leaf from the folio. Lay it onto the adhesive. Don't worry if it tears or cracks as it is applied. In fact, such fissures are desirable. Burnish the silver leaf with your fingers, making sure the leaf is in contact with the adhesive.

Tear away any loose large sections of silver leaf at the edges of the adhesive and reserve them. Using the small, stiff-bristled house-painting brush, brush vigorously over the silver leaf, flicking away any small excess pieces. This is a surprisingly messy job, producing fairy dust all over your work area.

Continue applying adhesive and silver leaf in sections until the full table is covered except for the top. Leave cracks and small gaps open, but patch any large gaps.

3 *Antiquing*

Optional: Antique the silver leaf to make the silver richer and to kill the brightness. In a small tub, mix together some pthalo green and Payne's gray paint to make a deep-green-black tone. Thin with water until the paint is a watery consistency. Start in an inconspicuous section of the table. Paint a section of the silver leaf with the thin paint.

Allow the paint to sit for about two minutes, then wipe away excess paint with a slightly dampened rag or paper towel. Leave a fine film of paint on the silver leaf, and leave paint in depressions and recessed areas. Continue, until all silver leaf has been antiqued. Allow to dry. Then paint all silver leaf with sealer.

4 *Mica gel*

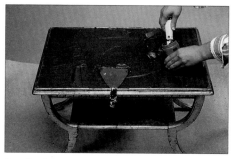

Apply the mica gel to the tabletop. Using the narrow paint scraper, scoop a blob of gel from the jar and plop it onto the tabletop. Continue until the jar is emptied. Spread the gel with the wide paint scraper, achieving an even depth of gel. The gel will shrink somewhat as it dries, so apply enough gel to make it nearly as thick as the recessed top.

When spreading the gel, avoid the temptation to try to make it completely smooth and flat, because that's impossible. Instead of fighting the natural textures that form from folding and smoothing the gel, continue working it until it is a satisfying overall texture.

5 *Embedding medallions*

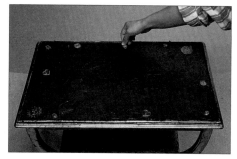

While the gel is still very wet, press medallions or other flat objects into the surface. The medallions can create an uneven surface, so you may wish to keep them near the edges of the tabletop, where they're not likely to topple glasses of red wine.

While the gel is still wet, look over the tabletop. Add or remove medallions and adjust the texture of the gel. If necessary, use a damp cloth to clean off any excess gel on the lip surrounding the top.

While the gel is still wet, use the narrow paint scraper to carve patterns or designs into the gel. Don't worry if you goof. Simply smooth out the gel again (removing and cleaning off the medallions if necessary) and start over.

Allow the gel to dry, two to three days.

6 *Rusted iron*

Optional: Add instant iron and instant rust. Using instant iron, paint the center section of the tabletop, following the directions on the jar. Allow to dry overnight.

Using a fine-point artist's brush, paint a design on the iron with the liquid instant rust. Apply a second coat if necessary. Allow to cure and dry. Some instructions on instant iron and rust suggest coating with a sealer, but sealer can obscure the effect of the rust and will also diminish the iridescent quality of the mica and the medallions. Try a test on paper or cardboard to see if you like the results before sealing the tabletop.

If your table has a top that is not recessed or is otherwise not suited to a studded-gel treatment, consider combining cut-out appliqués of sheet metal with stenciled motifs in metallic leaf. (See Art in Craft, page 80.)

Botanical Design

GRAPEVINES AND SOPHISTICATED COLOR
PRODUCE A CRAFTED CABINET

Nothing creates style quite like the melding of a rich palette with the textures
and forms of nature. Earthy olive green paint and gray-stained natural wood
complement the controlled chaos of grapevines artfully arranged over
laminated, parchment-thin golden grape leaves. The marriage of city
and country flavors makes this armoire adaptable to virtually
any room in either environment.

Read This First

Part of the pleasure of finishing this piece of furniture is the experience of finding and collecting leaves and vines. If grapevines are not available in your area, collect leaves that are a suitable shape and buy the vines from a florist or craft shop. Leaves must be pressed and dried for at least two weeks. If you do collect your own vines, do it in the summer or fall when the vines are pliable. Wear boots, long pants, and gloves – and watch out for poison ivy. Pull out good long lengths, the thicker the stem, the better. As you pull the vine down, wind and tie it into a coil, small enough to fit into a sink or laundry tub since the vines will later need soaking to rejuvenate them.

Collect leaves in the summer, if possible. By fall, grape leaves tend to be very fragile and thin. And fall colors aren't necessary because the leaves tend to change from green to a golden green-brown as they dry. While the leaves are drying, stain the cabinet's trim. Prime and paint the body with a base coat. If your armoire has a plastic laminate finish, use melamine paint for the base coat. (See *Melamine Paint,* page 27.)

BEFORE

An inexpensive unpainted wardrobe made of pine with very thin mahogany board panels can become a one-of-a-kind horticultural presence. All it needs are the right touches.

MATERIALS

- 2 dozen grape leaves
- scissors and a thick phone book
- 20 to 30 yd. (20 to 30 m) grapevines (allows for two vines on each side and two on the front, plus a generous portion for top arrangement)
- fine sandpaper (220 grade)
- pale- to medium-gray stain
- rag
- fine-point artist's brush
- easy-release painter's tape
- quart (litre) high-adhesion, water-based primer
- quart (litre) eggshell finish latex paint, deep olive green
- painting tools: paint brush, small roller, roller tray
- quart (litre) non-yellowing, water-based varnish
- paper towels
- carpet staples, small hammer
- garden clippers
- small quantity cellulose-based wallpaper paste

1 *Leaves*

Snip stems off the leaves and press them in a phone book. Leave about twenty pages between each page of leaves. Allow leaves to dry for at least two weeks.

2 *Vines*

Place a coil of vines in a bucket or sink and cover them with water. Soak the vines while the cabinet is being painted or for two hours.

3 *Staining trim*

Stain can be applied only to raw wood. (See *Staining Wood,* page 46.) Using fine sandpaper, lightly sand all areas that will be stained.

Remove doors and hardware. Place the doors on a tabletop and work on them while you work on the cabinet.

Stir the stain thoroughly. Using the artist's brush, apply stain along recessed trim or other hard-to-reach areas.

Using a rag or a paint brush, apply stain to the trim. Allow to dry.

4 *Painting panels*

Mask off all stained trim. Prime the panels and paint them with the deep olive green paint. (See *Painting Basics,* page 34.) Allow to dry.

Apply one coat of non-yellowing, water-based varnish to the stained areas of the armoire. Allow to dry, then repeat. Varnish can also be applied over the paint if desired. (See *Varnishing,* page 48.)

5 *Attaching vines*

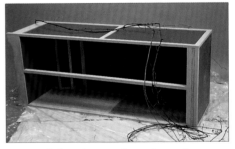

Unwind the vines and pat them dry with paper towels. When the armoire is thoroughly dry, lay it on its side. (If the armoire is heavy, recruit a helper.) Starting at the bottom of the armoire, arrange the vines onto the uppermost side.

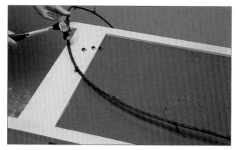

Starting at the bottom edge of the armoire, hammer carpet staples into the trim, anchoring the vine. Use as many staples as necessary to keep the vine reasonably close to the surface of the armoire.

Using garden clippers, cut the vine cleanly at the bottom edge of the armoire. Continue stapling the vine in place on the full side of the armoire. Don't cut off any excess vine at the top of the armoire.

Stand the armoire up (get help if needed) and arrange any trailing vines from the side along the top edge, stapling them in place. Don't allow them to hang in the door space. Otherwise, the door won't shut. Staple vines to the other side of the armoire and work any trailing vines into the top arrangement. Staple vines to the door panels, keeping them within the trim and working from a bottom corner to the opposite top corner.

6 *Laminating leaves*

Follow the instructions on the package of wallpaper paste to mix a small quantity.

Coat both sides of a leaf with the paste, leaving no dry spots.

Lay the leaf onto the surface of the armoire, aligning it with the vine. Smooth it from the center, eliminating any air pockets. Continue, pasting leaves on both sides of the armoire. The leaves may become wrinkly. The wrinkles will disappear as the leaves dry and shrink. Avoid trying to stretch the leaves flat. You will only damage the leaves.

7 *Doors*

Reattach the doors. Laminate leaves onto the doors. Allow both the vines and the leaves to dry.

8 *Varnishing*

Brush two coats of varnish over the leaves to protect them.

Branch management. If you wish to, provide your wardrobe with hardware fashioned from twigs. Choose live twigs freshly cut from a tree. Paint the cut ends with clear nail polish or varnish, and allow to dry for several weeks before sizing and attaching to your furniture.

Mad for Mosaic

CRAZY PAVING DISHES UP THREE FASCINATING TABLETOPS

Mosaic's history is cemented in Greek and Roman times, when magnificent pictures and designs were created from tiny tiles. But contemporary mosaic patterns, whether pictorial or abstract, can be created with combinations of whole or broken tiles, cutlery, marbles, jewelry, beads — even antique picture frames and lockets. Mosaics today not only mix texture, color and pattern, but also combine unlimited creative potential with hard-wearing permanence.

Read This First

Apply mosaic to a stable wooden tabletop, or cut a piece of plywood to fit the table. Many lumberyards will cut wood to your specifications, even circles. With its small irregular pieces, mosaic eliminates the precision work of cutting and fitting tile. The tile and crockery are smashed with a hammer (great therapy), and the pieces are placed to fit. Adhesives and grout are easy to use and virtually foolproof.

When collecting tile and other bits and pieces, decide ahead approximately which colors and textures you want. But be flexible. The serendipity of finding mismatched yet compatible pieces is inspiring. And don't worry if items aren't all exactly the same thickness. Some leveling can be done at the adhesive stage. Purchase *sanded floor grout,* not wall grout, in a color to complement the tile. Mosaic uses far more grout than tile, because the mosaic pieces are small, so buy at least double the recommended amount. Once the tile and grout choices are made, purchase paint in a coordinating color to paint the table's base.

MATERIALS

- fine sandpaper (220 grade) and tack cloth to degloss existing tabletop
- *if the table needs a top:* plywood, good one side, cut to fit your table (step 1); jigsaw, table saw; beam compass (or string, hammer and nail); pencil or pen
- primer and paint (step 2)
- tiles, crockery and other collectible items (marbles, glass beads, etc.)
- towel or rag
- hammer
- tile adhesive (either ready-mixed or the dry, mix-it-yourself kind)
- tongue depressor or similar disposable utensil
- sanded floor grout in the color desired (at least double the quantity specified on the package)

- small pail or bowl for mixing grout
- dropsheet
- rubber or plastic kitchen spatula
- plastic scrub pad or coarse rag, cloth
- *optional:* steel wool (for wrought iron)
- *optional:* power drill and large-diameter bit
- *optional:* bins for sorting tile pieces
- *optional:* grout sealer

BEFORE

Left, a table for two, in canary yellow with plenty of rust, needs some TLC.
Center, an interesting side table with that old tired look. But closer examination reveals elegant
lines, with the lip around the tabletop providing a perfect edge for mosaic.
Right, this new, small and rather expensive occasional table came with four quarry tiles set into
its top, one of which broke in transit. A new surface was needed.

AFTER

Left, a glossy-black border and fiddlehead pattern provide a sophisticated counterpoint to
earth-tone tile. The pattern is created from narrow border tile which, with its
consistent width, is excellent for composing linear designs.
Center, small, square, patterned accent tiles are arranged in a center block, with more smashed and
used as a border detail. Coordinating pieces of white tile fill the gap.
Right, this crockery mosaic combines plates, marbles, beads — and even the handle of a fork.
Crockery mosaics, because of their busy nature, are best when showcased
on a small table.

1 *Preparing the tabletop*

If your table has a top, sand it well to remove any loose or flaking varnish and to degloss any shiny areas, so that the adhesive will stick. Use a tack cloth to clean off all dust.

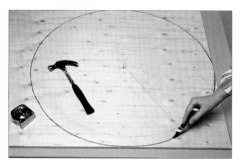

If the table has no top, cut one to size from plywood of the required thickness, ¼ in. (6 mm) if set into a small table, ½ in. (1.25 cm) for medium-sized tables, and ¾ in. (2 cm) for dining-sized tables. Many lumberyards provide a cutting service. If you're cutting the top, use a jigsaw for odd shapes or a table saw for straight edges. If the tabletop is circular, draw the circle with a beam compass. If you don't have a beam compass, hammer a small nail into the center of the board. Tie a string to the nail and, at the correct radius from the center, tie a pencil or pen. Holding the string taut and the pencil or pen straight up and down, draw a circle.

Cut along the line with a jigsaw.

Optional: Paint the underside of the tabletop (the good, smooth side of the plywood) with a coat of primer, then a coat of paint. Allow to dry.

2 *Painting*

If your table is wooden, prepare, prime and paint the base with either latex or spray paint. (See *Painting Basics,* page 34.) If your table has a plastic laminate finish, use melamine paint. (See *Melamine Paint,* page 27.)

If your table is wrought iron, clean it thoroughly, removing as much rust as possible with steel wool, and spray paint it with rust-covering spray paint. (See *Spray Painting,* page 44.)

Whatever type of table you have, do not paint the area to be tiled.

3 *Smashing tile*

Place the tile (or crockery), covered with a towel or rag, on a hard surface such as a concrete floor. Breaking tile on wood or another resilient surface is far more difficult.

Hit the tile (or crockery) with the hammer. After a few tries, you'll know how hard you need to hit to break things up. If you prefer to do your smashing without covering the materials, allowing greater control over the size of the pieces, *you must wear safety goggles.*

Continue breaking up the pieces of tile until they are a uniform, fairly small size, about an inch (2.5 cm) across. Sorting different color groups into different bins can help in the design process. Use care handling the broken pieces. Not only are the edges sharp, but the glaze on crockery and tile is actually glass. Small slivers of the glaze may break off and are difficult to see.

4 Planning mosaic

Plan your design. One by one, lay the tile and crockery pieces onto the tabletop, fitting the pieces onto the space. Leave a narrow gap, ⅛ to ¼ in. (3 to 6 mm), between each tile. This gap will later be filled with grout.

If making a crockery mosaic, set the pieces at random, or create some order by positioning like pieces together to form a block of color or perhaps a whole or partial shattered plate. Arrange all the pieces of the design in place, including any beads, marbles, jewelry and cutlery.

If creating a tile mosaic, mix both color and texture to create pattern. The design can be pictorial (sunflower, moon, stars, cat silhouette, rosebud) or abstract (pinwheels, zigzags, checkers, curlicues). Whole tiles can be worked in among the broken pieces, and borders can be formed.

5 Gluing mosaic

Use ready-mixed adhesive, or mix a small quantity of the dry adhesive with water according to the manufacturer's directions. Mix more as required. The adhesive should be the consistency of peanut butter.

Using a tongue depressor or similar stick, apply adhesive to the bottom of a mosaic piece. Cover the full underside of the mosaic piece, then put it back in its place on the tabletop. As you place it back, give it a little twist to ensure full contact of the adhesive with the tabletop. (If working on a crockery mosaic, glue all pieces except marbles and beads. See step 6.)

Start at one side or in a corner. With large surfaces, it's easy to lose track of which pieces have been glued. Place a ruler or stick across the table and work up to the stick. Then move the stick further along and work up to it again. Continue until all tiles are glued.

Keep the mosaics as level as possible. Add extra adhesive to the thin mosaic pieces in order to bring them up to the height of thicker ones. Allow the adhesive to dry and cure, a process that takes one or two days. Check the package directions for drying times.

6 Gluing marbles and beads

If working on a crockery mosaic, glue down everything except marbles or glass beads. Allow the adhesive to dry and cure. Using a power drill and a large drill bit, drill holes through the tabletop where the marbles are to be placed. Drill slowly and carefully, trying not to dislodge other pieces. If a piece pops off, glue it back on. Test the marble in the hole. It should sit lower than it did before, more level with the other mosaic pieces. If it is still too high, redrill the hole with a larger drill bit.

Spread some adhesive around the rim of the drilled hole, then place the marble or glass bead into the hole. Light from the drilled hole should illuminate the glass. Allow the adhesive to dry and cure.

7 Grouting

If you are applying mosaic to a large tabletop or a countertop, place the top onto its base now. Moving a large mosaic tabletop separately after grouting may cause grout to crack. Make sure the screws are the correct length and will not disturb the mosaic pieces.

Mix a small amount of grout. (A large batch will begin to dry while you're working.) It's easiest to work on small sections, unless two people are working together. Place four cups of warm water into a small pail or bowl. Add grout to the water until it has the consistency of heavy sour cream mixed with sand. If the grout is too wet, it will form hairline cracks when it dries. Too dry, and it will dry before you can work with it. Mix well. If the package directions call for slaking (allowing it to sit undisturbed), you must let the grout mixture sit for the required time.

Work over a dropsheet. This is a very messy job, resulting in a lot of grout crumbs and grout sand. Using a rubber or plastic kitchen spatula, spread grout over a section of the tiles, forcing it into the spaces between the tiles. If your table has a lip around the edge, fill up to the lip.

Fill all spaces, up to and including tiles attached to the cut edge of the plywood.

8 Removing excess grout

While the grout is still wet, sprinkle a dusting of dry grout onto the surface. This dusting will absorb some surface dampness, making the surface grout easier to remove.

Do not use any water in this step. Using a dry plastic scouring pad or a coarse rag, rub the surface of the tabletop, removing the excess grout and exposing the surface of the mosaics. The grout should fill the spaces between the tiles and be very close to level with the tops of the mosaic pieces.

It is tempting to use water to wash off the grout, but water is the enemy of grout. It will create hairline cracks as the grout dries.

Once the surface grout has been removed, wipe the surface of the mosaic clean with a slightly damp cloth.

Allow the grout to dry and cure while the table remains in place – don't move it. This stage will take two days. Never put leftover grout down the drain or into a toilet, unless you like to keep your plumber busy. Instead, place all leftover grout into household garbage.

9 *Finishing*

If the tabletop has not been reunited with its base, reattach it now.

If desired, apply grout sealer (available at tile stores) onto the grout. This product prevents the grout from absorbing stains.

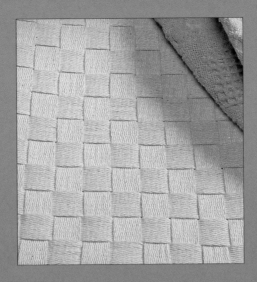

Seating

SITTING PRETTY WITH PROFESSIONALLY CRAFTED CUSHIONS AND SEATS

The seat of a chair is more than a place to park. Chair seats and cushions offer a design opportunity to add texture, color and pattern with fabric — along with a higher degree of comfort. Try to find an upholstery supplier that sells upholsterer's-quality high-density foam, batting, and dust-cover cloth. Dust-cover cloth is the non-fraying fabric that goes under the seat to cover raw edges and bare plywood. If you can, take along the plywood base from the old cushion as a pattern, and have the foam pieces cut to fit.

Following are instructions for a basic seat cushion, a piped seat cushion, and a woven webbing seat, along with two treatments for backrest cushions — tailored and shirred. Only the piped cushion requires sewing.

Above, the chair on the left has a basic seat cushion and a shirred backrest cushion. The chair on the right has a piped seat cushion. *Left,* both chairs have basic seat cushions and tailored backrest cushions.

Basic Seat Cushion

Read This First

This seat cushion is the type that looks like a large soft cookie. Use this treatment primarily on round chair seats. Square seats tend to look better with a straight-sided or piped cushion. Choose the thickness of the foam, between one and two inches (2.5 to 5 cm), depending on the style of the chair. If the thicker foam will obscure detailing or be ungainly in height, choose a thinner foam. It will look better, but the trade-off will be a harder chair and slightly less comfort for those sitting on it. Buy plywood that is good one side. This means that one side has a smooth finish, while the other is knotty and rough. The good side of the plywood will be positioned down on the seat. (Good both sides, which is much more expensive, is not necessary.)

MATERIALS

- plywood, ½ in. (1.25 cm) thick, good one side, cut to fit the seat of the chair
- high-density upholstery foam, 1 to 2 in (2.5 to 5 cm) thick, cut to fit plywood
- fabric, 8 in. (20 cm) larger than the plywood both in length and in width
- iron
- ruler and marker
- scissors
- batting, 6 in. (15 cm) larger than the plywood both in length and in width
- stapler and ⅜ in. (1 cm) staples
- non-fraying upholstery dust-cover cloth (enough to cover the plywood)
- screws (to reattach cushion to chair), screwdriver
- *optional:* jigsaw
- *optional:* spray glue; scrap paper or dropsheet
- *optional:* lining (step 5)

1 Getting started

Remove the fabric and foam from the underlying plywood. Clean the plywood as thoroughly as possible, removing any mold and staples.

If the old plywood is beyond salvation, have a new piece cut or cut one yourself with a jigsaw. The new plywood should be ½ in. (1.25 cm) thick, good one side.

Have a piece of high-density upholstery foam cut to match the size and shape of the plywood.

2 Cutting fabric

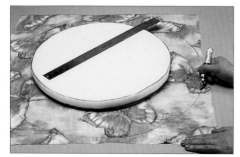

Iron the fabric.

Lay the foam or the plywood onto the wrong side of the fabric. Measure and mark the fabric 4 in. (10 cm) from the edge of the foam. Do this at regular intervals around the perimeter of the foam. Join the marks to make a continuous solid line.

Cut along the line.

3 Laminating foam to plywood

Optional: Gluing the foam to the plywood can reduce slippage. Lay down some scrap paper or a dropsheet and place the foam onto it. Check the directions on the spray-glue label for making a permanent bond. Spray the foam with glue.

Lay the rough side of the plywood on the gluey foam, centering it.

4 Batting

Lay the plywood/foam onto the batting. Lift the batting up, against the side of the foam, marking the batting at the top edge of the foam. Do this all the around the foam.

Cut the batting along the marked line.

Optional: With the plywood/foam centered on the circle of batting, foam-side-down, spray-glue a section of the overhanging batting. Fold the glued section up onto the foam. Repeat until the batting is glued to the perimeter of the foam.

5 *Stapling*

If the cushion fabric is lightweight, cut a lining from a woven material such as broadcloth. Lay the fabric face-down, with the lining on top.

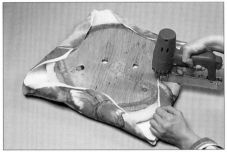

Position the plywood/foam/batting sandwich, batting-side-down, onto the center of the fabric. Gently but firmly, pull and staple the fabric to the plywood in four places, equal distances apart.

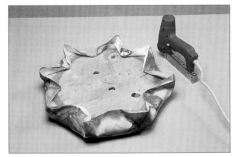

Gently but firmly, pull and staple the fabric to the plywood between each of the four staples, keeping the pressure even.

Gently but firmly, pull and staple the fabric to the plywood between each of the eight staples, keeping the pressure even.

Gently but firmly, pull and staple the fabric to the plywood between the staples. Continue until the fabric is stapled evenly all around.

6 *Finishing*

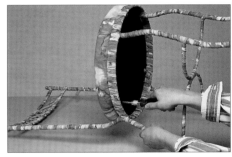

Cut a circle of dust-cover cloth slightly larger than the circle of staples, but smaller than the bottom of the cushion. Staple it to the bottom of the cushion, starting with four equidistant staples. Then staple between them, as you did to staple the cushion fabric, until the full perimeter is stapled.

Reattach the cushion to the chair by screwing appropriately sized screws into the seat frame and the plywood of the cushion. Work from underneath the seat.

Piped Seat Cushion

Read This First

Making a piped seat cushion takes some planning and sewing ability, although the sewing is actually basic and straightforward. The piping gives the cushion an elegant, crisp finish. Piping is available in braids or wovens, and it comes in a wide range of colors, prints and finishes, from shiny to matte. Choose a piping that will coordinate with the fabric, yet stand out enough to accentuate the tailored edge. If you have never sewn piping with a piping foot on your sewing machine, here's a chance to try it and see how professional the results are. The sewing goes faster and is easier if a piping foot is used. It keeps the piping on track and the sewing uniform. If a piping foot is not available, use a zipper foot.

MATERIALS

- plywood, ½ in. (1.25 cm) thick, good one side, cut to fit the seat of the chair
- high-density upholstery foam, 2 in. (5 cm) thick, cut to match the plywood
- paper, pencil, ruler
- fabric, approx. ½ yd. (.5 m) for each cushion
- scissors
- piping (measure perimeter of cushion and add 6 in. (15 cm))
- dressmaker's pins
- sewing machine with piping foot
- thread to match fabric
- batting, 6 in. (15 cm) larger than the plywood both in length and in width
- stapler and ⅜ in. (1 cm) staples
- non-fraying upholstery dust-cover cloth (enough to cover the plywood)
- screws (to reattach cushion to chair), screwdriver
- *optional:* jigsaw
- *optional:* zipper foot
- *optional:* spray glue; scrap paper or drop-sheet

1 *Getting started*

Remove the fabric and foam from the underlying plywood. Clean the plywood as thoroughly as possible, removing any mold and staples.

If the old plywood is beyond repair, have a new piece cut or cut one yourself with a jigsaw. The new plywood should be ½ in. (1.25 cm) thick, good one side.

Have a piece of high-density upholstery foam, 2 in. (5 cm) thick, professionally cut to match the size and shape of the plywood.

2 *Drafting a pattern*

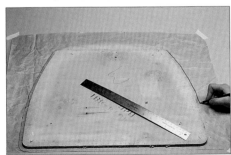

Make a pattern for the top of the cushion cover. Lay the plywood onto paper and trace closely around it. Using a ruler, measure and mark a ½ in. (1.25 cm) seam allowance from the plywood edge all around the perimeter. Then join the marks to create a cutting line.

3 *Cutting fabric*

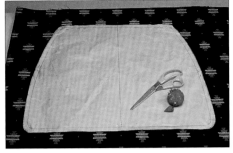

Cut out the pattern and lay it onto the fabric, centering it carefully onto the fabric's design. If the design printed on the fabric is directional (vines climbing a trellis, for example), it should run from the front of the cushion "up" to the back.

On fabric with a geometric pattern, the placement should match for all cushions. Pin the pattern in place and cut out the fabric for all cushions.

For the sides of the cushion cover, cut strips of fabric, 6 in. (15 cm) wide, across the width of the fabric. Cut the strips to match up with the fabric design of the cushion tops, taking into consideration the width of seam allowances. Usually, one width of fabric will circle one cushion.

4 *Sewing*

Starting at the center-back of the cushion top, pin piping on the right side of the fabric, matching the raw edge of the piping to the cut edge of the fabric. Check that the piping has a ½ in. (1.25 cm) seam allowance. If not, compensate. Pin well. At corners, clip into the seam allowance of the piping, allowing it to bend. At the start and the end, allow 2 in. (5 cm) extra piping, laying the ends across the seam allowance.

Attach the piping foot to the sewing machine. With matching thread, begin at the center-back and sew the piping in place, ½ in. (1.25 cm) from the cut edge.

Lay a cut strip of fabric onto the piped edge of the cushion, with right sides together, matching the pattern along the front edge of the cushion. The ends of the strip should join at the center back. Pin the strip to the cushion top, starting at the center-front and working out, until the strip is pinned to the full perimeter of the cushion top. Clip the seam allowance of the strip at corners, if necessary. If the strip is too short, sew an additional section to the strip.

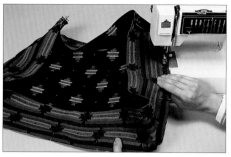

With the piping foot still in place, sew the strip tightly against the piping. Join the ends of the strip. Turn the cushion cover right-side-out and inspect the seam. Resew any gaps.

5 *Batting*

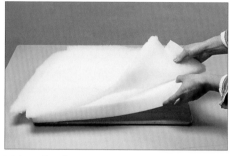

Using the foam as a guide, cut a piece of batting 3 in. (7.5 cm) larger all around (or measure and cut batting as shown on page 156, step 4). Lay the foam onto the plywood and the batting onto the foam. Notch the corners, so they dovetail when bent down over the sides of foam.

Optional: Gluing the foam to the plywood and the batting to the foam can reduce slippage. (See *Basic Seat Cushion*, steps 3 and 4, page 116.)

If you opt not to glue the plywood and the batting to the foam, lay the foam onto the rough side of the plywood and center the batting over the foam.

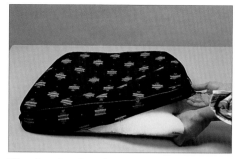

Slip the piped cushion top over the batting.

6 *Stapling*

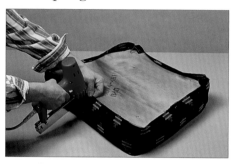

Turn the cushion upside-down. At the center of each side, gently but firmly pull the fabric to the back of the cushion and staple in place.

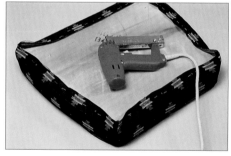

Continue, adding staples equally to all sides, keeping the tension even. Don't staple one full side before going on to the next. This will cause uneven tension and ripples.

Finish corners by stapling the center of the corner, then folding and stapling the excess down, like a fan, on both sides. Do several small folds to avoid puckering.

7 *Finishing*

Cut a piece of dust-cover cloth to fit the bottom of the cushion. It should cover the staples but be within the edge of the cushion. Staple it in place with one staple centered on each side. Work out from these staples, stapling all around the edge.

Reattach the cushion to the chair by screwing in appropriately sized screws from the bottom of the seat.

Woven Seat

Read This First

This technique is for replacing a worn-out webbing or split-cane seat. The seat must have the necessary dowel-like four rungs: front, back and sides. Purchase webbing at an upholstery supply store or buy wicking for oil lamps. The wicking shown here was bought at a hardware store in a 25 yard (23 m) roll for a surprisingly modest price. The wicking is a flatly woven natural cotton of a pleasing width. But why stop here? Many cast-off items can be used to great effect. Layers of ribbon, bunched yarn, or ends of trims can be used. Torn rags, tied end to end, could give a folksy, rag-rug feeling to a seat. Once started, stick to this project until finished (it only takes a few hours), so you won't lose track of the weaving.

MATERIALS

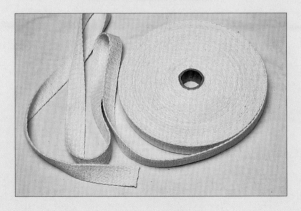

- approx. 20 yd. (20 m) wicking (the type used for oil lamps) or webbing about 1 in. (2.5 cm) wide (amount required can vary, depending on size of chair seat)
- stiff cardboard, 3 x 6 in. (7.5 x 15 cm)
- ruler and marker
- stir stick or other narrow stick, to fit the width of the seat
- white carpenter's glue and tape, or stapler and ¼ in. (.5 cm) staples
- *optional:* needle and thread for sewing webbing ends

1 *Getting started*

Cut a rectangle of stiff cardboard, about 3 x 6 in. (7.5 x 15 cm). Wrap the webbing around the length of the cardboard from end to end to make a shuttle. Don't cut the webbing.

Mark the center points on the front and back rungs of the seat. The markings will help you keep the weaving straight, especially if the rungs are different lengths.

2 *The first pass*

Stand in front, facing the chair. Begin on the left side. Glue and tape (or staple) the webbing to the left-side rung. (Glue, tape and staples will be hidden by the weaving.)

Slip the shuttle under the back rung, then bring it up and over the back rung and toward the front, keeping the webbing flat.

Bring the shuttle forward, passing over the front rung, then under the chair seat to the back, and over the back rung again.

Keep the webbing even, neat and tight.

Continue until the full seat is covered, ending on top at the front right corner.

3 *Weaving*

Slip the shuttle under the seat to the back right. Bring it up, over the back rung, then under the right-side rung.

Weave the first row by bringing the shuttle over the right rung. Pass it *over the first strip* of webbing and under the second. Continue this over-under motion across the full width.

Using a ruler (or stir stick, as shown here), prop up the alternating strips under which you will pass. When you finish a row, remove the stick and reposition it for the next row. This will make the weaving easier and help you to avoid errors.

Turn the chair upside-down and weave across the back of the seat, as you did for the front.

Turn the chair right-side-up again. Reposition the ruler or stick. Weave the second row by bringing the shuttle up over the right-side rung. Pass the shuttle *under the first strip* and over the second. Then continue across the full width of the seat.

4 *Weaving, continued*

Continue in this manner, alternating the over-under weaving pattern. Stop to check the pattern occasionally. Keep the weaving tight by pushing it together with the tip of the ruler or stick.

About halfway through the weaving, the shuttle may not fit through between the webbing. Take the webbing off the shuttle and pull it through in a loosely gathered bunch.

If the webbing isn't long enough and you need to join it, sew the ends together on the underside of the seat and tuck in any loose ends.

5 *Finishing*

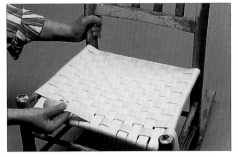

Weave to the last row.

On the underside, weave halfway across the last row. Then cut the webbing and glue (or sew) the end down, tucking away any excess.

Backrest Cushions

Read This First

The decision to have a tailored or a shirred cushion on the seat's backrest is based on the style of the chair. A tailored cushion doesn't stand out. It is an integral part of the design of the chair. A shirred cushion, in contrast, commands attention. It makes a statement, giving the chair a showy, fashion-conscious sensibility. A tailored backrest cushion can be made from any type of fabric. A shirred backrest should be made from lightweight, finely woven fabric. The backrest can be finished decoratively with braid trim on the back side to hide staples, or by carefully gluing the finishing panel in place for a clean, crisp look.

MATERIALS

- plywood, ½ in. (1.25 cm) thick, good one side, to fit chair back (If the backrest is curved, reserve plywood from existing cushion.)
- high-density upholstery foam, 1 in. (2.5 cm) thick, cut to match the shape of the plywood
- fabric (To determine yardage, see step 2.)
- tape measure
- batting, 4 in. (10 cm) larger than the plywood both in length and in width
- stapler and ⅜ in. (1 cm) staples
- *for shirred cushion:* needle and thread
- hot-glue gun
- *for trimmed back:* 2 yd. (2 m) braid trim, 2 small pieces of tape
- dressmaker's pins
- screws (to reattach seat to chair), screwdriver
- small amount of paint to match fabric (for heads of screws)
- utility knife or X-acto knife
- *optional:* spray glue; scrap paper or dropsheet

1 Getting started

For all cushions: Remove the fabric and foam from the underlying plywood. Clean the plywood as thoroughly as possible, removing any mold and staples.

Have a piece of high-density upholstery foam, 1 in. (2.5 cm) thick, cut to match the size and shape of the plywood. Although it is best to have the foam professionally cut, foam this thin can be cut with scissors.

2 Cutting fabric

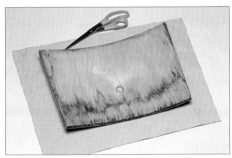

For tailored cushions: Lay the foam (or the plywood) onto the wrong side of the fabric. If the design printed on the fabric is directional (vines climbing a wall, for example), it should run up, from bottom of backrest to top. Measure and mark a cutting line 3 in. (7.5 cm) from the foam. Do this around the full perimeter. Cut along the line.

For shirred cushions: Measure the deepest section of the plywood backrest. Add 5 in. (12.5 cm). Cut fabric to this depth and to double the width of the backrest. Set the fabric aside.

For all cushions: Cut a piece of fabric 1 in. (2.5 cm) larger on all sides than the foam. This will be used to cover the back of the backrest cushion. If the design printed on the fabric is directional (vines climbing a wall, for example), it should run up, from bottom of backrest to top. Set the fabric aside.

3 Cutting batting, gluing foam

For all cushions: Cut batting 1½ in. (4 cm) larger on all sides than the foam. Notch the corners of the batting so that they dovetail when the batting is folded over the sides of the foam. Set the batting aside.

Optional: Gluing the foam to the plywood can reduce slippage. Lay down some scrap paper or a dropsheet and place the foam onto it. Check the directions on the spray-glue label for making a permanent bond. Spray the foam with glue.

Lay the gluey side of the foam onto the front side of the plywood.

4 Gluing batting

For all cushions. Optional: Lay the plywood and foam, foam-side-down, onto the batting. Using the spray glue, spray a section of the overhanging batting and fold the glued section up onto the side of the foam and plywood. Repeat until the batting is glued to the edges of the foam all the way around.

5 *Shirring*

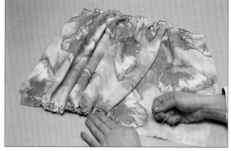

For shirred cushions: By machine or by hand, sew along the top and bottom edges of the fabric and gather to the width of the seat back, plus 5 in. (12.5 cm).

6 *Stapling*

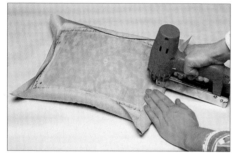

For tailored cushions: Lay the fabric face-down. Center the plywood/foam/batting section, batting-side-down, onto the wrong side of the fabric. Gently but firmly, pull the fabric onto the plywood and attach with one staple centered on each side.

7 *Stapling, continued*

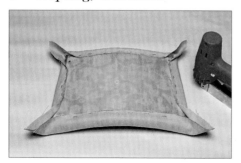

For tailored cushions: Work around the cushion, adding staples equally on all sides. Keep the pressure even.

For shirred cushions: Don't staple the fabric at the sides yet, only at the top and bottom.

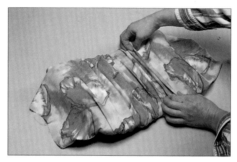

Occasionally turn the cushion to the front side and organize the gathers.

Staple the sides, with the fabric pulled taut. Pulling the fabric too tightly will disturb the gathers.

8 *Corners*

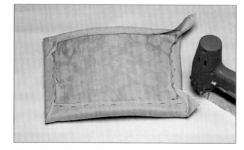

For all cushions: To make a neat corner, cut the point off the corner. Tuck one point into the overlap. Then fold the remaining point under. Staple in place.

9 *Finishing*

For all cushions: Find the fabric set aside for covering the back of the cushion. Fold and press the edges 2 in. (5 cm) to the wrong side.

To make a neat corner, notch the corner nearly to the crease. Fold one edge flat. Then fold the other edge over it, tucking the corner under.

For a flat finish: Heat up the glue gun. *Be careful not to burn your fingers, especially if you are not experienced with a glue gun.* The glue becomes hot enough to cause deep burns, and the glue sticks and keeps burning.

Position the fabric, centered onto the back of the cushion, right-side-up. Pin at the corners. Unpin and lift one corner. With the glue gun at high heat, squeeze a narrow, neat bead just inside the folded edge of the fabric. Lay the corner down, allow the glue to cool and lift the next corner. Repeat until the back is glued on all the way around.

10 *Finishing, continued*

For a trimmed finish: Plug in the glue gun. Lay the fabric centered onto the back of the cushion, right-side-up. Staple the fabric to the back of the cushion, centering one staple on each of the four sides. Staples must be carefully placed at the edge of the fold of the fabric. Otherwise, they will not be covered by the trim. Work out from the positioning staples equally, stapling along the edges of the fabric on all four sides.

Wrap a small piece of tape around the end of the braid to prevent fraying. Carefully apply hot glue to the taped end of the braid, then slip this end under the edge of the fabric between two staples, hiding the tape. Working in sections, apply a bead of hot glue to the underside of the braid and lay the braid glue-side-down, hiding the staples and the folded edge of the fabric.

When the braid is glued on all the way around, cut it with 1 in. (2.5 cm) excess. Tape around the end. Apply glue to the end and tuck it into the gap with the other end, keeping the join as invisible as possible.

11 *Reattaching cushions*

For all cushions: In a color compatible with the fabric, paint the heads of the screws to be used for reattaching the seat.

Position the seat back into the chair. Mark where the screw holes will go.

Using a sharp utility knife or X-acto knife, cut a tiny hole at each of the marks. The cut should break only one or two threads, allowing the screws to pass through the fabric. If these holes are not cut, the fabric will bunch when the screws are screwed in.

Position the seat back in place and screw in the screws.

Joy von Tiedemann

SHEILA McGRAW began her career painting sets and designing props for major high-fashion retailers. She then moved into the highly competitive world of freelance illustration, producing art for newspapers, magazines, advertising and package design. Next she turned to illustrating children's books. Her first book, Robert Munsch's *Love You Forever,* became an international bestseller that reached number one on the *New York Times* Children's Bestseller List.

An avid home sewer, decorator and painter, she has written numerous craft books, including *Papier-Mâché for Kids,* a bestseller that won the prestigious Benjamin Franklin Award. Her books on painted and decorated furniture have firmly established her as one of the foremost writers in the field. Sheila McGraw lives on a farm north of Toronto and is the mother of three grown sons.

BOOKS WRITTEN BY SHEILA McGRAW

Papier-Mâché Today; Papier-Mâché for Kids;
Soft Toys to Sew; Gifts Kids Can Make;
Dolls Kids Can Make; Pussycats Everywhere;
This Old New House; Painting and Decorating Furniture;
Decorating Furniture: Antique and Country Paint Projects; Decorating
Furniture: Découpage, Paint and Fabric Projects; Decorating Furniture: Stencil,
Paint and Block Print Projects; Decorating Furniture: Texture,
Paint, Ornament and Mosaic Projects

BOOKS ILLUSTRATED BY SHEILA McGRAW

Love You Forever, I Promise I'll Find You, Lightning Bug Thunder